Devil's Toy Box

By

Joni Mayhan

Devils Toy Box. Copyright 2015 by Joni Mayhan. All rights reserved. No part of this book may be used or reproduced in any manner without written permission from the author.

This is a true story, however some of the names have been changed or omitted to respect their privacy. Any resemblances to actual places, people (living or dead), or incidents that happened that are not listed are purely coincidental. Prior written approval has been obtained from all parties who are mentioned in this book.

Also by Joni Mayhan:

Lightning Strikes (Angels of Ember Dystopian Trilogy– Book 1)
Ember Rain (Angels of Ember Dystopian Trilogy – Book 2)
Angel Storm (Angels of Ember Dystopian Trilogy – Book 3)

The Soul Collector

Bones in The Basement: Surviving the S.K. Pierce Haunted Victorian Mansion

Devil's Toy Box

Ghostly Defenses – A Sensitive's Guide for Protection

The Spirit Board (Winter Woods – Book 1)
The Labyrinth (Winter Woods – Book 2)
The Corvus (Winter Woods – Book 3)

Acknowledgements

This was one of the hardest books I've ever written. In order to compose it, I had to open several doors that I had long ago nailed shut and bricked over. Bringing up the past was difficult, but I wanted to share my story.

Even though I changed a few names and omitted others for the sake of their privacy, this is a true story. While it was painful to endure, I'm glad it happened because it led me to the place I am today. My impressions of the events that transpired are mine alone. While I did reach out to the parties involved in the book for input, my recollections are the way I felt at the moment and are transcribed from the multiple diaries I kept during the period.

Thank you to everyone involved, from the people who lived this from the inside out to the beta readers who diligently picked up another book shortly after the last one was published. I couldn't have done this without any of you.

My wonderful beta readers: Rosa McRae, Cara Keene, Gare Allen, Barb Wright and Alex Zaccheo. You've saved me so many times. If I ever make it big, I'm booking a cruise for all of us to celebrate!

And finally, thank you to my children Laura and Trevor. You were both so young when this happened. Keeping you safe was always my top priority. I'm glad we all made it through.

Joni

1

There wasn't anything unusual about the house. At first glance, it was as normal as any other house in the suburban central Massachusetts neighborhood. Small and blue, it was shaped like a box with windows and doors. It was the type of house where you might envision window boxes overflowing with brightly colored geraniums and a festive garden flag that said *welcome!*

Nothing about it suggested it was haunted.

We pulled up and simply stared at it for a moment, our hearts plunging to the depths of disappointment.

In the past two years, we had saved every penny possible for a down payment. Renting an apartment seemed like such a waste, considering we could be putting our money towards an investment in our future.

We'd already spent most of the day driving around town looking at houses that our overzealous realtor had mistakenly shown us. Unfortunately, most of them were far outside our price range. I don't know if it was wishful thinking on her part, or if she truly made a mathematical mistake, but once we caught it, the damage was already done. It would be difficult to settle for less than we expected. We sat in front of the small blue house with little enthusiasm. *This* was what we could afford.

I had already mentally decorated another house across town, the one with the gleaming hardwood floors and the built-in bookcases that would nearly fit my growing book collection. There were three bedrooms and a sunroom, where I would put a chase lounge, pots filled with ferny green plants and a spindly-legged secretary desk where I would finally write my novel. We would add a big square coffee table, one that would hold the entire Sunday paper, and a comfortable recliner for my husband to lounge on.

The house in front of us had none of that.

"Okay," my husband said. "We might as well take a look."

We can always add on.

He said that at the last house, the one with double the square footage. At this rate, we'd have to add on a whole other house just to break even.

I gave him a tight-lipped smile and got out of the car.

It was 1989. I was twenty-five years old, happily married, and was pregnant with my first child. All my dreams were coming together in one fell swoop.

We'll just make do, I thought to myself. Besides, it was better than renting an apartment.

The landlord at our apartment was slow to make repairs and the space wasn't suitable for a baby. It only had one bedroom and steep stairs that led to a landing that couldn't be gated. I was also anxious to get out of Ayer.

While we initially loved the town of Ayer, Massachusetts, with its quaint downtown area and bevy of parks, it was quickly losing its luster. Since the nearby military base was closing, the town was becoming a ghost town, something I had no interest in living in. Compounding the situation was a change in jobs for my husband, bringing him farther away each day.

In our pursuit of new locations, we happened upon the town of Westborough. The downtown area didn't have the same charm that Ayer's had, but it was more convenient. It had a great school system, plenty of shopping, and was closer to my husband's work. He also pointed out that it was a good investment property, since the housing market was beginning to boom in the area.

We pulled ourselves out of our warm cars, taking in the brown grass and naked trees. Winter was settling in, which didn't help the curb appeal of the house in front of us.

A gust of sharp wintry air blew across the lawn, sending a Styrofoam cup someone must have tossed from a car window sailing end over end. It came to rest at the chipped concrete steps.

"Let's take a look. Shall we?" the realtor asked, putting on a fake smile. She put her key in the lockbox, but struggled to get it open, a sure sign that the house hadn't been shown in a while. The box was practically rusted shut.

I gave my husband a sidelong glance.

"Give it a chance," he whispered to me.

Once the realtor got the door unlocked, she held it open for us, giving us a polite smile. We'd been all over town in the past few hours and she was eager to either make a sale or cut us loose.

I went in first, crinkling my nose as the odor hit me squarely in the face. It smelled unsavory and stagnant, like a combination of liver, onions, and wet dog, mixed in with the radiant aroma of a greasy sofa that was ten years past its prime. The hardwood floors were scuffed and scarred and there wasn't a single built-in in sight.

"This is a fixer upper, but it's in a great neighborhood," she told us, as though she was able to wipe the olfactory assault from our memory banks. "Give it a fresh coat of paint and add your own furniture, and I'm sure it will look much different."

I wasn't so easily sold. The entire house had a neglected feel to it, with cracked linoleum floors in the kitchen and outdated wallpaper in many of the rooms. I arched my eyebrows as I lifted a section of the linoleum with my foot, displaying a soggy subfloor.

"We can replace that," my husband was quick to point out. He was an adept handyman, which would be needed in a house like this. I was having a difficult time adopting his enthusiasm. It was nothing like the house of my dreams.

I was forever a daydreamer with sky-high goals. I wanted to be a writer, sitting at home cranking out best sellers while my adorable children played nearby. This certainly wasn't the place I imagined doing it in.

My husband must have caught my thought.

"Once you sell a few best sellers, we'll upgrade," he said with a smile. I only hoped he was right. This was miles away from my version of happily ever after.

I followed the long hallway, feeling my stomach sink with every room. It was far from perfect. In fact, it was so far away from perfect, it was almost miserable, but it was all we could afford.

The two bedrooms at the end of the hall were small, but manageable. One would be our bedroom, while the other would be a nursery for our baby. I cradled my stomach thinking about the life inside of me. I couldn't wait to finally be a mother. It was all I thought about for the last few years.

This would be the place where we could start building our lives, I thought with a wistful smile.

The odd man who owned the house was parked on the greasy sofa the second time we came to see it. His lack of enthusiasm was appalling. He flipped through the channels on his television set, barely looking up to answer our questions. The most we got from him was that he'd lived there for seven years, spending the last year and a half alone. His wife and children had moved out ahead of him, waiting for him to sell the house and then join him. It should have been the first sign that things were amiss.

After a month of difficulties, we finally signed on the dotted line and were given the keys to what would soon become our own private hell.

If we only knew what awaited us, we wouldn't have been quite so happy.

(Above) The house just after we purchased it

2

The rooms echoed as we walked through them, armed with disinfectant and sponges. I took some measure of gratification in the sound, knowing that we would quickly replace the emptiness with the sounds of our growing family.

There was so much work ahead of us first, though. After the previous owner moved his possessions out, it was apparent the house was neglected for more than a decade. He did no more than a quick cleaning prior to placing the house up for sale.

The chimney was filthy, the gutters were packed with leaves, and the roof was showing signs of age. The furnace was on its last leg and the hot water heater wasn't far behind. If he did one thing to maintain the house, I couldn't find it.

The first job I tackled was cleaning. I was intent upon eradicating all the nasty smells, essentially erasing the prior owners presence from the house altogether.

It wasn't an easy task.

The walls were bare, except for the pale rectangles where pictures must have hung for decades, looking like ghosts against the filthy wall. The stove was crusted with years of spilled food, and the refrigerator was black with mold.

We promptly hauled the appliances to the town dump and replaced them with new models. My husband ripped up the old linoleum and replaced it with something we picked out together. We really wanted ceramic tile, but it just wasn't in our budget yet. The initial investment had nearly wiped us out.

The walls were painted with neutral colors, erasing all the ghostly rectangles, and the yellowed ceilings were given a fresh coat of white paint to cover up the years of nicotine stains.

We covered the scarred floors with carpeting. I loved the look of hardwood floors, but we wanted something softer for our baby. Carpeting would provide her with a much easier landing spot when she was learning to walk. We also needed to paint the windowsills, but not before we removed a full inch of accumulated dust and dead flies.

The moving truck was coming in a few days, which didn't give us a lot of time to get the house ready. As I went into the front bedroom, armed with paper towels and window cleaner to work on the first window, I got a peculiar feeling. It felt as though someone was standing behind me. I swiveled around, fully expecting to find my husband in the doorway, but the room was empty.

"Honey?" I called.

My voice echoed in the empty room.

The hair on the back of my neck prickled.

I strained my ears, trying to pick up the faintest clue of what I felt. All I could hear was the sound of my own ears ringing.

Curious, I walked into the long hallway that separated the bedrooms from the kitchen and living room spaces, my footsteps sounding hollow in the silence. As I reached the living room, I caught a glimpse of movement out the front window. My husband was leaning against the mailbox, chatting with one of our new neighbors.

"Hmmm," I murmured to myself. Maybe it was just my imagination. I didn't think about it again until I went down into the basement.

I wanted to find the box packed with towels so I wouldn't waste so many paper towels on the dirty windowsills. I had already gone through a half roll on the first window. As I came down the narrow wooden stairs, I felt a fluttering in my chest. Something didn't feel right down there.

I paused on the stairs, allowing my eyes to adjust. The basement was a typical New England cellar. It was the kind of place you'd park a washer and dryer, eyeing the shadows as you hurried from the safety of the stairs to the circle of light glowing from the bare bulb on the ceiling. It was dirt-crusted and moldy. Cobwebs draped from the bare rafters like garland. I nicknamed it the "Freddy Kruger Basement," after the character in one of my favorite horror movies because it felt like a place where someone might store their demons.

My husband laughed off my concerns, telling me he thought it would make a great family room one day. I wasn't so convinced. The space gave me the willies.

The basement was long and narrow with a door and two windows on one end. The other end was perpetually lost in darkness, which always made me nervous. Somewhere between the two zones sat an old workbench.

It was scuffed and stained, looking as though it had lingered untouched in the shadows for the past forty years. The wood was softened at the edges, worn smooth by decades of use. As I stared at it, an image came into my mind of an older man leaning against it, hammering on a piece of metal. He sensed me watching him and turned to glare in my direction.

I pressed my eyes shut, my heart hammering wildly as I willed the image to go away.

I hadn't had a psychic impression in many years and I didn't want to start again.

The last time I had one, I was seventeen years old, living in my father's haunted house.

Please don't let it start again, I pleaded before heading upstairs, the box of towels long forgotten.

3

I saw my first ghost when I was seven years old.
For nearly a year beforehand, I watched the shadows
in my room move as soon as my mother turned off the
light. I would lay there, transfixed by what I was seeing.
It made no sense.

I waved my hand above my head, trying to see if I
was causing the movement, but my shadow didn't
penetrate the darkness. I didn't know what it was until I
started having nightmares to accompany it.

The nightmares came on like a thunderstorm,
pinning me to the bed as they repeated over and over
again, like a movie clip set to repeat. In the dreams, I
found myself in the middle of the woods, in a place I'd
never been before. Somewhere in the darkness a shadow
man was chasing me.

He was tall and skinny with arms that nearly
touched the ground. His legs were long and spindly, as
well, reminding me of an alien I once saw in a movie. He
wore a long black trench coat and top hat that hid his
face from view. All I could see was the fringe of unkempt
black hair and eyes that glowed a demonic red.

Every time I thought I escaped him, he caught up to
me again. I ran, my breath coming in jagged pulls. The
dream was so vivid, I could feel the sweat cooling on my
forehead and the uneven ground beneath my feet,
making my ankles twist. I ran until I came to an old barn
sitting beside a dirt road.

A large dusk-to-dawn light mounted on a telephone
pole cast an amber glow just outside the barn. I
remember thinking that if it were summer, the light
would be filled with dancing moths and June bugs. We

had one of those lights in front of my dad's shed and sometimes we could see bats diving in to catch the bugs.

Near the doorway to the old barn was a ski lift that led up a dark mountain. I didn't question why the ski lift was moving without anyone there to operate it. I just jumped onto one of the seats and hung on, watching the barn grow smaller and smaller below me.

I made it halfway up the hill. The darkness was nearly complete, surrounding me like a blanket, blotting out even the midnight stars that should have shone above me. Then, I heard a voice in my ear.

Come with us.

I jerked around, searching the darkness, not finding anyone.

"No!" I screamed.

His breath was in my ear, fetid and sour, as though he recently chewed on a mouthful of carrion.

Come with us or we will take your family, one by one.

I struggled to move away, but I had nowhere to go. Beneath me, the earth had faded into the darkness. If I jumped, I'd plummet to my death.

"No! Leave me alone!" I screamed again.

We'll start with your little sister. She will be most delicious.

And then we'll take your mother, and then your father, while we make you watch.

I opened my mouth to scream, and the nightmare fell away. In its place was my bedroom, the same as it was before.

I peered out the doorway to the dark hallway beyond it, hearing the distinct sound of ringing. The sound grew louder and louder, nearly splitting my skull until it simply stopped.

I had the same dream four nights in a row.

On the fifth night, when I awoke and stared out into the dark hallway, it wasn't empty.

A misty white shape lurked there.

I sat up in bed, tugging the covers up to my chin. As I watched it, my ears began ringing again. The sound was like smoke alarms going off inside my head, growing louder as the apparition walked closer.

I attempted to scream, but my voice was frozen.

I watched in horror as it drifted closer and closer, until it finally reached my bed.

Come with us.

The same voice from my dream rang in my head.

"Noooooo!" I screamed repeatedly until my mother raced down the hallway.

As she approached the doorway, the shape disappeared, but I knew it wouldn't be gone for long.

It probably wasn't a coincidence that my parents began fighting during this time. I could hear the sounds of their arguing as I lay in bed each night.

I sometimes wondered if the ghost in my room was to blame. He sometimes made me feel angry for no reason at all. Was he doing the same thing to my parents?

They divorced shortly afterwards and I went to live with my mother in another town.

After that last ghostly experience, it was as if a door was kicked opened in my mind, allowing the dead to enter freely. I continued to sense ghosts all the way through my childhood. They would congregate at the corners of the room, peering at me with a mixture of emotions. Many of them were lost souls, hanging at the fringes of our human existence like stray dogs looking for scraps. I felt sorry for them, but there wasn't anything I could do for them.

12

The sad ones usually left me alone. It was the angry ones that scared me. They stalked me through the day, following me home where they could prey on me during the night.

The moment the lights were turned off, I could feel them moving in closer. I pressed my eyes closed, willing them to disappear, terrified at what I was seeing and feeling. I couldn't shut out the ear ringing, though. The shrill sound moved through the room, following me like a wayward shadow. If I was lucky, I fell asleep and left them behind. If I wasn't lucky, they followed me into my dreams and tormented me all night long.

The ear ringing became nearly maddening. I quickly discovered that the sound wasn't a constant. It varied as I moved around the room. It was almost as though I was tracking something invisible.

I once asked a friend if she could hear the tone too, and she gave me a questioning look.

"What tone," she asked.

"Ghost sounds," I told her, happy to finally share my secret.

She arched an eyebrow and threw my words back at me with an edge of disbelief. "Ghost sounds?" she said. The next day, she told all the kids at school how I thought I could hear ghosts. They laughed and began calling me names.

People who heard tones weren't that different from people who heard voices in their heads. I knew I wasn't crazy, but explaining what I was feeling often lumped me into that same category. When I tried to tell my family about the ghost in my doorway, they were quick to tell me that it was just a dream.

There's no such thing as ghosts, they told me.

I learned to keep it to myself after that.

It was a secret I would live with for most of my life.

By the time I was a teenager, I nearly forgot about the ghost in my old bedroom.

I was going through my own internal conflict. If there were ghosts nearby, I didn't notice them and they didn't care enough to let themselves be known.

I think everyone goes through growing pains as a teenager and mine were no different. I was rebellious, angry, and tired of being held back. My mother and I fought constantly over every little thing, and I grew weary of the battles. One day, after an especially nasty fight, I packed my bags and moved in with my father and stepmother, back into the house where I grew up.

The move required me to change schools in my junior year of high school and uprooted my entire life, but I needed a change. I was ready for something new.

The kids at my old school were street-wise and rebellious. I fell in the wrong crowd and found myself in a world of alcohol and drugs that wasn't a comfortable fit. The new school was different. The kids were wholesome farm kids, the same ones I went to grade school with before moving away after the divorce. They welcomed me back as though they actually had missed me, and I quickly began rebuilding my life.

After I settled in, I was shocked to discover that my father's house was still haunted.

My bedroom was at the top of a long dark flight of stairs. I stood at the bottom, listening to the sound of my ears ringing. I wanted to blame it on tinnitus, but I couldn't. With the ringing came the image of the cloaked man with the glowing red eyes. He stood at the top of the stairs, willing me to join him.

Come with us.

I was rooted to the floor with fear. I wanted to race out of the house and keep running until the sound was gone, but I couldn't.

This was a new start. I had to get through it.

Besides, I couldn't just turn around and go back to my mother's house. I had conveniently burnt that bridge when I stomped out of her house in the middle of the night. I had nowhere else to go.

I flipped on the light at the base of the stairs and chased away some of the shadows, my heart beating a mile a minute.

I stared wide-eyed at the landing, making out the dark walnut paneling and the shadows that lurked in the corners. The house was cavernous and dark. Being a traditional A-frame, it only sported windows at either end, leaving a long stretch of darkness between the two.

"Just leave me alone," I hissed under my breath.

Nothing happened, so I took a deep breath and walked up the steps, trying to ignore the panic that weakened my knees.

"Be brave. Just be brave," I whispered to myself.

I made it to the top without issue and went into my room, feeling bolstered by the result. If I did it once, I could do it again. I would just have to learn how to live with it. There weren't any other options.

It was almost as though he gave me a pass for my first time up the stairs. Maybe he was impressed that I grew up, putting my fears behind me. Or maybe, he hungered to find a new way to scare me since I outgrew all his old tricks.

It wouldn't be the last time I encountered him.

It was as though he was pacing himself. He allowed me the luxury of relaxing before he pounced on me, scaring me to the tips of my toes.

I walked down the stairs, counting them in my head to keep my mind occupied, and felt the brush of a hand against my neck. Other times, it was a whispered breath against my ear.

One thing that bothered me was the way he phrased the statement. Come with us. Even though I was only hearing one voice, he spoke as though there were more of them.

Was he the chosen spokesperson?

Did that mean there was an entire army of ghosts out there vying for my soul?

The thought made me shudder.

I wasn't there more than a month before he upped the ante three-fold. He started making noises at night. The sound was so loud; it brought me out of a deep sleep.

I sat up in bed, searching the shadows, half expecting him to pop out at me, but the room was still and silent. The sounds were coming from above me.

I stared at the ceiling as thought I could see through the floor, wondering what was going on up there.

My father said the house sometimes creaked and groaned from settling, but that wasn't what I was hearing.

The noise sounded again and I recognized it as the shift of cardboard boxes sliding across the floor. One after another moved above me.

There was no doubt I was awake. Nobody could tell me that I was dreaming this time. I listened to the sounds three nights in a row before I finally decided to do something about it.

I slipped from my bed and tiptoed to the attic door. As soon as my fingers closed in on the doorknob, the noises stopped. I flipped on the light and walked up, my legs trembling beneath me. I was shocked at what I saw.

Nothing was out of place.

I looked around, almost expecting to see something emerge from the shadows, but nothing moved.

I retreated to my bedroom, where I tossed and turned for the rest of the night as my mind chewed on what I experienced.

What could cause boxes to move on their own?

If it wasn't a ghost, then what was it?

I told my dad and step-mom about it the next morning, but they didn't have any suggestions either. It wasn't rats or we would have seen the droppings. My father walked around and looked, but he didn't find anything.

The rest of the encounters were usually minor. I heard doors open and close while I waited for my parents to come home from work. Footsteps often marched across the second floor above me when I was home alone in the house. When I walked past the attic door, it would sometimes slam shut, as if pulled from the inside by a ghostly hand. The last encounter I had was prior to my senior prom.

My date was going to pick me up at five o'clock, so I set aside a full hour to get ready.

I was excited about going to the prom. It was the first prom I had the opportunity to attend. After spending most of my teenage years watching other people go out on dates, while I sat home by myself, I was actually going to the prom myself.

I picked out a beautiful, but simple dress. It was white with tiny pink flowers and a deep sweetheart neckline. My mother gave me a pretty necklace to wear with it, along with a pair of strappy high-heeled sandals.

I felt like Cinderella as I got ready. My dress hung on the back of the bathroom door while I fixed my hair and applied my makeup, and I couldn't stop looking at it, imagining the magical night in front of me.

My parents weren't home from work yet, so I had the entire house to myself.

I showered and dried my hair, putting on my favorite lotion so my skin was soft and fragrant. I began rolling my hair in my electric rollers, hoping my hair would mirror my mental image of what prom hair should look like. It was thin, brown, and ordinary, often prone to bad moments. Electric rollers would either drastically improve it or would send me back to the shower to start all over again. I had barely rolled one strand of hair when it sounded as though every shelf in the closet behind me fell.

The crashing sound went on for an eternity. I heard glass bottles breaking and tiny bits of glass tinkling down through the refuge. I fully expected to open the closet door and discover collapsed shelves, with all my stepmother's perfumes, shampoos, and lotions in a broken pile on the bottom. What I saw made me gasp.

Everything was in its place. Nothing was broken.

My heart nearly froze in my chest. All I wanted to do was run.

I bolted outside to sit in my car, wearing nothing more than my slip and the one roller in my hair.

I watched the windows for several long moments, daring something to move. If it had, I would have roared down the driveway, abandoning all notions of my senior prom, but after fifteen minutes, nothing had moved. I tentatively tiptoed back inside and finished getting ready in a matter of minutes

I moved out of the house three weeks later.
Was it happening all over again?

4

I really needed something good to happen to us, or maybe more specifically, I needed something good to happen to *me*.

It felt like my entire life up to that point was filled with uncertainty. I watched my friends graduate from high school and go surefooted out into the world, starting new grown-up jobs or enrolling in prestigious colleges. I just couldn't find anything that stuck.

I knew I didn't want to follow in my parent's footsteps and work at the factory they labored at their entire lives, coming home with the best parts of them already used up. They stumbled through the evenings, simply going through the motions until it was time to do it all over again the next day. I didn't want a job where I lived for the weekends. I wanted to live every day.

The problem was figuring out how to do that.

I tried college, but I couldn't find a comfortable fit there either. I felt like a square peg trying to shove myself into a round hole. I knew what I wanted to do, but getting there wasn't an easy matter. I wanted to be a writer. A novelist.

I spent a lot of time daydreaming out the window, imaging how my life would be. I would purge out novel after novel, spending my free time at our ocean estate, playing with our children. We would have wonderful friends and neighbors who would invite us over for dinner parties and barbeques. We would take fabulous vacations to warm locations and drink fruity drinks with umbrellas. So far, my life couldn't be farther from that.

When we lived in Indiana, we had our electricity turned off so many times, we learned to live without it for long periods at a time. We were both working two part time jobs in addition to carrying full time class loads, but we just weren't making any progress. After a lengthy discussion, we picked up our things and moved a thousand miles east to Massachusetts where my husband's family lived. It was supposed to be a new start for us.

I came to know a lot about new starts.

They seldom came with all the promise and glitter you thought they did. Instead, they came with a lot of uncertainty and anguish. They came with missing the people you left behind, knowing there are some things you couldn't replace.

You might be able to buy new furniture and new dishes, but you only got one mother and one father and mine were back home in Indiana like a distant memory.

Holidays became brutal as I sat around someone else's family table, eating someone else's stuffing. I missed my family more than I thought I would.

I felt lost without them.

We started out our new lives in New England by renting the top floor of the old house in Ayer, but after two years, we had the itch to find a place of our own. I kept thinking about the house on the ocean that I had always dreamed of, but reality would be a much different concept. If I was going to make it as a novelist, it would be years in the future. In the meantime, I had to work my forty hours a week to help pay the rent, the electricity, and the other bills that came along with being a grown-up.

Here I was, twenty-five, married, pregnant, and standing in my own house. It wasn't the ocean estate, but it was a starting place. I always saw myself as an optimist. This was where we would start out, I told myself, and then planned to make the best of it.

My husband's family helped us move our belongings into the house. What would have taken most people all day, only took us one morning. One trip in a rented truck and we had everything relocated from one place to another. I looked around at our worn out furniture, sitting in the living room against the freshly painted walls and took a deep breath.

It was a starting place.

"Buddy! Sheba! Wanna go outside?" I said, calling out the words that usually made our two dogs go wild, but the house remained silent.

"Buddy?" I tried again.

After a few seconds, Buddy appeared at the top of the stairs, wagging the tip of his tail like he did when he was nervous.

Buddy and Sheba were Shetland Sheepdogs, better known as miniature collies. Buddy was a purebred, while Sheba was a mix between a Sheltie and a Golden Retriever, making her the larger of the two.

They were happy dogs who were always eager to please us. In the seven years we owned them, they never once displayed fear about anything, with the exception of the vacuum cleaner.

Both dogs were graduates of obedience training. Having spent several years working in the pet industry, I knew the advantages of having well-trained dogs. All it usually took was a well-spoken command and they would do as they were asked, but Buddy flat out refused to come to the basement.

"Come on, baby," I cooed to him, but he just stood at the top of the stairs, wagging his tail between his legs and whining.

I wasn't sure what I was going to do. He was twenty-five pounds, which was far more than I could carry in my current state, but I needed to get him outside to relieve himself. The door to the basement led directly to the backyard.

"Sheba?" I tried. Sometimes I could use peer pressure to convince one dog to get the ball rolling. If Sheba ran down, then hopefully Buddy would follow.

Unfortunately, Sheba didn't even make an appearance at the top of the stairs. I tried for a few more minutes before giving up and letting them out the kitchen door upstairs. It was closer to the street, which worried me, but it was going to be the only way to get them outside. It was apparent we were going to have to build a fence around the property.

I sighed, looking around at everything that still needed to be done. It was a never-ending job.

Welcome to the world of home ownership.

I smiled to myself, trying to buffer my emotions with optimism, something I was growing more adept at.

The house had good bones. It was something we could definitely work with. I had a checklist in my mind of things I wanted to tackle, starting with removing the horrible wallpaper in the kitchen and bathroom. It was outdated and speckled with filth. I scrubbed the kitchen wallpaper with bleach and water, but it still looked dirty. It almost looked as though someone had thrown food against the walls and just left it.

I hated to feel such distain about the former owners, but I couldn't help it as I encountered the mess they left behind. It would take a lot of hard work to get it back up to par, but I was confident we could do it.

"We'll make it work," I whispered to myself.

The first night in our new house should have been a great night.

I was happily married to my best friend. I was pregnant with a baby that was going to make us a family, and I was sleeping in my own house. Something wasn't right though. I could feel it niggling at my mind, like a door left unlocked. I pulled my heavy body from the bed, rolling sideways until my feet hit the floor.

Navigating with a baby inside of me wasn't easy. It threw off my balance and made me feel thick and sluggish. I wasn't one of those women who loved being pregnant. It was something I endured for the sake of bringing another life into the world. I couldn't wait until it was over and I could have my body back again.

I felt like a turtle, carrying my shell in front of me.

The thought made me smile, but it didn't ease my mind.

The hallway was dark, with only the soft glow of the kitchen nightlight lighting my way. I took a step out into the hallway and paused. The baby began moving around inside me. I felt a sharp kick land in my ribs and winced with the sensation.

Something wasn't right, but I couldn't figure it out. I decided to make a quick pass through the house and check the doors to insure they were locked.

The new carpeting muffled my footsteps, but the old floorboards beneath them gave me away with every step, squeaking softly in the silence of the sleeping house. I found my way into the dining room and stopped to look around.

The kitchen and dining room were separated by an L-shaped counter, with a small table on one side and room to cook on the other. A long wall to my right separated the kitchen from the living room.

Our old cast-off furniture looked strange in the space, bringing a sense of home to the room. Most of what we had was handed down from family members, giving us an odd assortment of mismatched pieces. I loved them though. They were comfortable and worn in all the right places, fitting my body like a pair of broken-in jeans. I wandered into the living room and plopped down on the couch, where I could look out the picture window at the street beyond our front yard.

The idea for a book tickled the back of my mind. The idea seemed effortless. While my baby slept, I would write. When she was awake, I'd spend every moment adoring her. By the time she took her first step, I'd have a book completed, and we could begin to reap the benefits.

A floorboard creaked behind me and I turned, expecting to see my husband in the hallway, sleepy and confused as to why I was sitting on the couch in the middle of the night. Instead, I just found an empty room. The dogs were locked away in their crate in the bedroom and the cat was asleep on the other end of the couch beside me.

My ears began to ring as well, but I pushed it aside. Nothing was going to interrupt my newfound happiness. I got up from the couch, checked all the door locks, and then headed back to bed.

I wasn't asleep for five minutes before I found myself in a familiar dream.

I was on a ski lift, heading up into a dark unknown. *Come with us.*

The voice murmured in my ear, sending me flying out of bed.

I made it halfway across the room before my husband caught me and woke me up.

"Nooooo!" I screamed, fighting him off.

He held my arms and shook me gently awake. "Shhhh...Joni, you were walking in your sleep again," he said. "Come back to bed."

As I eased back into the tangle of covers, I tucked my hand protectively around my stomach.

I wouldn't let anything happen to my baby.

No matter what.

5

I first began walking in my sleep around the same time I started sensing ghosts. I was never sure if the two were interlinked or were merely coincidental.

The sleepwalking always started with a nightmare and ended with me waking up in an unusual place, usually with terrified people surrounding me, staring at me with wide eyes. I would slowly come around, like a patient waking from anesthesia, the details of the nightmare slipped fleetingly from my grasp.

My family told me how I ran through the house, screaming at the top of my lungs. They chased me until they caught me and then watched me stare back at them with glazed, terrified eyes. They said it was almost as if I was seeing people who weren't there. I looked at my mother, then at my father, and finally at the space between them as though someone else was standing there. They shook me and called my name until my eyes slowly sharpened to awareness.

Even though I normally just ran down the stairs to the living room, they were worried that I'd make my way outside. We had a pond in our front yard, and I knew from their whispered conversations that they were worried I'd somehow find my way to the water. I was a fairly strong swimmer, but would that carry into my sleeping state? What would happen if I just continued to walk? We lived in the middle of forty acres of farmland and wooded terrain. If I walked in the right direction for long enough, I would be difficult to find.

My parent's marriage began dissolving at the same time I started sleepwalking. I lay in bed and listen to the sounds of their voices rising. Angry words would spill from their bodies, barbs meant to maim and harm the other. I wanted nothing more than to run downstairs and ask them to stop, but I knew it wouldn't do any good. Their anger was too blistering hot to cool, especially by the hand of a child.

The negativity became as real as the walls around us. I could walk into a room and feel the energy swirling as though an electric current filled the air. That energy must have sunk into the wood, allowing the house to absorb it like oil into dry wood. The man in my nightmares probably enjoyed it, as well. I could imagine it feeding him. He would suck it in with a deep breathe, smiling the satiated grin of a man who just devoured a feast.

The sleepwalking was soon followed by blinding migraine headaches. It was as though my head was collapsing under the pressure, like a roof piled with too many feet of snow.

The doctors were stupefied. Most people who suffer from migraines begin getting them when they hit puberty, but I got mine at eight years-old. In every essence of the word, they followed the pattern of classic migraines. They came on slowly, wrapping spiked talons around my skull until I buckled under the mercy of the pain. I retreated to a dark, quiet room, where nothing but sleep would bring me relief.

"It must be from the divorce," people whispered.

My parents separated during this time and everyone was looking for a place to assign the blame.

My mother brought me to the hospital where specialists wired me up to various machines to measure my brain activity. I had CT scans, EEGs, X-rays, and sessions with a chiropractor. At the hospital, they drew my blood, checked my eyes and my spine. They even admitted me into the hospital for a week for a variety of testing, but came up with nothing to explain the migraines.

The medication they put me on made me fall asleep during class, so they tried something else. It didn't work either, which led to something else, which eventually led to them throwing up their hands and suggesting that I might grow out of them.

They came on around lunchtime and by noon, my head was nearly ready to explode. When they were at their worst, I had two or three attacks each week. I wouldn't emerge from my room until the next morning, feeling weak and trembling. Then at night, I would sleepwalk. It was either one or the other.

My mother usually heard me as I bolted from my room as if being chased by a legion of zombies. I'd hit the wall on my way down the stairs, sometimes screaming at the top of my lungs. Most of the time when my mother finally caught me, I woke up, remembering little of the event. Other times, it took a bit more effort.

After seeing the movie *Jaws*, I ran through the house for nearly an hour, screaming. My mother tried to shake me awake, and when that wouldn't work, she threw a cup of water in my face. I woke up shortly afterwards, the image of severed heads floating in the water filling my mind. After this, she cut me off from anything macabre or even remotely scary. Gone were the creepy comic books, the scary movies, and even cartoons that had an element of horror. I was no longer allowed to watch *Scooby Doo* and my *Nancy Drew* books were removed from my room. If it helped or not, it wouldn't last for long. I would sleepwalk for the rest of my life.

Having it happen during pregnancy was unnerving on several levels.

Firstly, I needed to get as much sleep as possible, considering I was carrying around a growing baby. The other reason was obvious. I might hurt myself and the baby during my midnight flights of fear.

I asked my OB-GYN about it and she thought that the increased hormones might have something to do with it. She suggested that my husband stopped trying to stop me, but to follow me instead. What I didn't tell them about was the nightmares that accompanied the sleepwalking.

The man on the ski lift was back, the spokesperson for all that was dead and evil.

Come with us.

This time, it wasn't my younger sister he wanted. It was my unborn child.

(Above) the basement prior to the remodel

<u>6</u>

We spent the first few months in our new house trying to make it our own. I sewed curtains for all the windows and hung pictures in places where I thought they'd look the best.

My husband had a never-ending punch list to attend to and kept himself busy with home improvement projects.

As I stood at the kitchen sink, I looked out the window at the lawn behind the house, my mind wandering.

The voice in my dream was familiar, yet it wasn't. Was it the same entity who tormented me in my youth or something altogether new?

I almost hoped it was the same one. If it was a new one, it meant he was pulling my thoughts out of my head. The concept was thought provoking and more than a little terrifying. If he could read my mind, he'd know in an instant what scares me.

On November 15th, my daughter made her way into the world. It was a time of celebration and exhaustion. My days and nights were consumed by her every waking need. My writing dreams faded away like a distant memory. All I could think about was this amazing baby in front of me.

The sleepwalking ceased, mainly because I wasn't getting enough sleep to be able to manage it. Laura was up every two hours all night long. I would carry her into the living room, sit in my rattan rocking chair and rock her for hours.

I stared out the window, watching the moon trace a path across the star scattered sky, wondering about life in general. It was astounding to me that we had created another human being, one I grew inside my very own body. It was the most amazing miracle, something I'd never take for granted.

No one could have prepared me for what it was like to be a new mother. It was such a bounty of emotions; I couldn't put them all in one place. I felt an overwhelming sense of love for this tiny human. Even though I had only known her for a matter of weeks, I would have sacrificed my own life for her, if needed.

I loved her even though she flailed, red-faced and inconsolable, during the night, not calming down until miles were traced up and down the hallway. I bounced her on her stomach, trying to relieve trapped gas, even though it never seemed to help. I changed her diaper, even when it wasn't wet. I fed her until she pulled away with anger. There just wasn't anything I could do to make her happy. She spoke a language I didn't understand, one made up of shrieks and tears, one that tore my heart right down the middle with jagged strokes.

The pediatrician gave it a title. He called it colic, which placed it in that mysterious category that could have included a dozen or more ailments.

People were helpful with their suggestions, but none of them seemed to make a difference.

They suggested that she was reacting to something I was eating and it transferred to my breast milk. I reduced myself down to the blandest of diets, but it did no more good than the walking down the hallway did.

They told me to take her for a ride in the car to settle her down. I tried it several times and it worked like a charm until we got back home and she woke up screaming. Was it something else? Something no one would even begin to consider.

I began looking around the house, examining the shadows.

Someone gave us an old mirror that had been in my husband's family for generations. It was gilded gold, with ornate swirls and a pitted surface that made it both homely and beautiful at the same time. I considered the history that it held in its wooden painted frame, the number of faces that had peered into the glass over the past hundred years. I wondered how many of them were young women with crying babies, finding their own eyes in the depths of the glass, trying to find answers buried somewhere even deeper.

I hung it on the wall in the living room beside the door, thinking that it would be nice to have a mirror there to check my appearance before I answered the door, if anyone ever bothered to ring the doorbell. The truth was: I was isolated. I didn't have any friends in Massachusetts and the only people I knew were from work, a place I left behind to raise my baby. Most of the time, I used the mirror to entertain Laura. We would stand in front of it and stare at our reflections. I made funny faces at her, trying to get her to smile. She would smile back at me for a moment before something caught her attention over my shoulder, something I couldn't see.

I turned with a gasp, only to find the room empty.

Colic on its own was a horrible infliction, but I wondered how many first-time mothers endured the challenge in a haunted house. How much of what was happening was truly medical and how much was paranormal? This wasn't a theory I shared with anyone, but I didn't push it aside.

I thought about it a great deal. I stared at the shadows, wondering if someone was staring back.

The ghost was still there. I could feel him hovering in the hallway, as though he was standing at the doorway watching her sleep. When she woke in the middle of the night, my ears would ring like crazy as I rushed into her room to rescue her from the horrible thing that made her cry. Had he been in her room watching her sleep? Was he waking her up?

I felt a little bewildered. Motherhood was nothing like it was on television. Even my daughter wasn't what I had expected.

I thought she would have been blond like me with a sweet demeanor. I had an unrealistic image of us, probably garnered from a magazine photo, sitting in a field of flowers, smiling at one another with love and admiration. She would coo at me, knowing instinctively that I was the person who cherished her most. She would reach for me when she awoke in the mornings, a smile lighting her face. She was the love of my life, but she was none any of those things.

She was born with dark curly hair like her father, and a determination I couldn't fathom. There was intelligence in her eyes that went beyond her handful of days on the earth. It was almost as though she was born with many lives already behind her. She had us figured out well before we figured her out. I spent every day just marveling over her when I wasn't battling with her instead.

By the time she was six months old, my entire life had changed. If my focus had once been my husband, it was now my daughter. It was so transcending, it was as though it had always been that way. I could not look at him and rouse up the emotional ties we had once shared. It was now all about her. I took every ounce of love and adoration and I greedily gave it all to her. I did not have any time for him.

Darkness had descended on us, something that came on so slowly we didn't notice it until it was covering us whole. I was sleep-deprived most of the time and all of my attention was focused on my baby. I spent the day yearning for another hour of sleep that would never come. My days were spent with dirty diapers, frequent feedings, housework, and pet care. There wasn't a moment when I could just put her down for a nap and get some work done because she wouldn't nap. I did what I could with her on my hip, but it was far more difficult than I would have ever imagined. My husband would come home after a full day of work, exhausted and numb.

I watched him glance around at the messy house, his mouth a thin flat line, as he asked me what I did all day. Gone was the loving tone that he once used with me. In its place was a measure of distain and judgment. While I craved having a partner to share in my grief, I became an opponent instead.

The way we handled these early days would set a tone for the remainder of our relationship. Instead of teaming up together and conquering the problem, like we had always done in the past, we cast blame. We couldn't see beyond our own diminished satisfaction. We found fault in the other for putting us in this position.

For him, I'm sure a lot of it was due to my fractured love. I took the one-hundred percent that I once gave to him, and I reduced it down to a sliver. It became so thin, you could hold it up to the light and see right through it. I didn't have the time or the energy to produce enough devotion for both of them. If I had to choose, it would go to the one who needed it the most: my baby. I could not seem to make him understand just how exhausting this new life was for me.

How could I explain my day to anyone?

The days ran together, separated by two-hour nightly jags, where I never even managed to reach REM sleep before being woken by a screaming baby.

I came into her room to find her staring at the corner, tears flowing freely down her cheeks. I searched the room, wondering what she was seeing. Was something waking her up? Or was this just normal infant behavior?

I picked her up from her bed and held her close to me, feeling the warmth of her body merge with mine. Her crying gasps eased slowly, followed by hiccups until she was back to normal. She searched my face with her wide blue eyes, as if asking me a question she didn't yet have words for.

"Did you have a nightmare?" I asked her, putting my nose into the whirl of hair on the crown of her head. I carried her back to my bed for the next few hours, too afraid to sleep for fear I'd smother her with my own body. I would just lay there and watch her sleep, her tiny fists moving with the pattern of her dreams.

"You're spoiling her," people told me when I complained about her lack of napping. "Just put her down and let her cry it out."

I tried, but after twenty minutes, I couldn't take any more.

Nothing interested her for long. I learned to do the dishes and run the vacuum with one arm. Someone gave us a baby walker, which was helpful. It was nothing more than an infant seat on wheels, with a wide tray that stretched out in front of her. I could put her in it and throw a handful of toys on the tray, which would occupy her for at least fifteen minutes, giving me a chance to catch up with household chores so I didn't get *the look* when my husband came home from work.

I made my way through the days, feeling slow-witted and sluggish. When she was finished with the walker, there was nothing else I could do to occupy her. If I set her down for more than a minute, she began to cry, wanting to be held again. I found myself nodding off while she played on the floor in front of me, waking in terror that she'd crawled past me to the open doorway.

Every time I looked at the gaping doorways, my blood nearly boiled.

My husband had removed all the doors inside the house when we first moved in. After we had carpeting installed on top of the hardwood floors, the doors were too tall to slide across the carpeting. He pulled them all off and stacked them in the garage, promising to cut several inches off the bottoms before rehanging them. But life got busy, as it usually did, and the doors remained in the basement for nearly a year. It added an element of danger to my days and drove another wedge between me and my husband.

One afternoon, I was in the kitchen putting away groceries. I plopped Laura in her walker and turned my back for several seconds to grab a bag off the counter. As I turned, I caught sight of her sailing down the hallway towards the open basement door.

She was moving far faster than she should have moved on her own. It was almost as if she were being pushed by an invisible hand.

With a gasp, I dropped the bag and ran towards her, catching the edge of the walker as the first wheel went over the threshold to the basement stairs.

"Oh my God," I whispered through my tears, as I pulled her out of the walker.

I held her close to me, breathing in the scent of her and realizing just how close I'd come to losing her. If I hadn't turned when I did, she would have fallen down the stairs.

The negative energy swirled around me, taking advantage of my diminished state of mine, and latched onto me eagerly. The loving man I'd married became my opponent. Blame became something we flung at one another, hoping to inflict injury. When he came home at the end of the day and looked around, as if inspecting my work, I heard the voice in my head urging my anger.

He has no right to judge you.

He doesn't know what you went through today.

He didn't hang the doors and your daughter almost died because of it.

I screamed at him about the doors, something I never did before. I became a raging, red-faced version of my normally calm self. Gone was the hesitant, eager-to-please young woman. In her place was a person who felt nothing more than blinding fury.

As if feeling my anger, Laura began to wail in my arms, her face growing as red as mine.

"She could have died because of you!" I screamed.

He didn't respond, but in his face I saw defiance.

Maybe if you'd spend more time watching the baby instead of sitting on your ass, this wouldn't have happened.

The words came to me freely, as if I was reading his thoughts.

"You have no idea what I go through every day!" I screamed.

I was never adept at arguing with him. He always thought of a dozen clever things to say, while my responses always came to me hours later after the argument had long passed. In my diminished state, I

38

couldn't rise above the red-hot anger that fired through my veins. My baby could have died.

This time, he wouldn't fight me. He took the screaming baby out of my arms and promised to hang the doors the following weekend, which he did, but it wasn't enough. I began to distance myself from him. I stopped sharing the details of my day with him, began resenting him when he came home without offering to take the baby for a moment to give me a break.

He thinks you're lazy.

He thinks you just sit around all day watching soap operas.

The words were not my own, but I didn't question them. They came to me through the dim fogginess that had become my every day existence, and I accepted them as the truth. What I didn't realize was that they were not my own words and they weren't his either.

Someone was in the house, and he was enjoying the fun.

He hadn't had fresh people to manipulate since he'd driven out the last family.

He wouldn't stop until he bled us dry.

Nothing would ever be the same again.

(Above) Joni with Laura and Joni's mother, Charlotte.

7

By the time the first year passed, motherhood had changed me in a way I never thought possible.

While my life now had a deeper purpose, I became more aware of the dangers in the world. I stopped looking at life through rose-colored glasses, but began seeing it as a place filled with hazards. There was so much going on around us that could cause us harm.

I worried about raising a child in a world filled with anger. The Gulf War broke out when Laura was nine months-old. We sat in front of the television, stunned at the images on the screen. How could we raise a child in a world filled with such hatred? Would it change the way the world functioned as a whole? My thoughts turned towards the future. What if this led to even more wars?

The fall of Saigon came when I was just eleven years old, but I was already aware of the impact it had on our culture. I saw men camped out on street corners, begging for money with signs that said "Vietnam Vet," and I understood from an early age that war changed people.

The things they saw could not be unseen. The damage went so deep, the scars became more prevalent than the tissue surrounding them. We once had a neighbor who was a Vietnam Vet and it took him over, like a deadly infliction. He never left his house, spending long hours in his parent's basement, listening to music. If a car backfired on the street, he hit the ground, his mind returning to the days of war. Was this the kind of world I wanted my daughter to grow up in?

What if the war extended to our shores? What would happen if we lived with the same fears our parents' endured during the end of World War II? Would we all build bomb shelters in our backyards, watching the news constantly, searching for new threats?

I tucked her closer and promised to do my best to keep her safe.

This wouldn't always be easy. Even the turmoil in the world wouldn't compare to the havoc we would experience inside our own home.

As Laura began sleeping through the night, my sleep deprivation faded and I began coming back to myself. I became selfish of my precious minutes of free time. After being denied for so long, I began painting and writing again, two things that set my soul free. I also became more aware of what was going on around me.

The months of unrest had left me with half my senses intact. Once I began to function again, the entity returned to the forefront of my consciousness.

It started softly, with a minor instance here and there, followed by long periods of inactivity, leaving me to believe it was just my imagination.

The reprises were just long enough to make me wonder if it was gone. I began to question my sanity and the decisions that had led me to believe we had a haunting to begin with. After all, I hadn't seen anything. If our house was truly haunted, wouldn't I have seen the ghost by now?

I started reevaluating the abilities I had always lived with. Was my ear ringing a sign that something was there? Or was it tinnitus, like my parents told me when I was a child? As much as I wanted to believe the latter, the entity wouldn't allow me such notions.

I began feeling as though I was being watched again.

When the awareness came over me, I first searched for normal explanations. I looked around the room, expecting to find my husband home early from work. When that wasn't the case, I turned towards the window. Was someone peeping in at me?

Thick foliage separated our house from the other houses. If someone was out there, he was standing in the middle of briar-laced woodland. I pulled the blind anyway, trying to chase away the maddening feeling.

I hated being alone in the house all of a sudden. When I felt as though I was being watched, I would go to another room, often leaving a basket of laundry unfolded on the bed or a bag of dirty diapers parked near the hamper. I didn't know what else to do.

I resented the chill that climbed my spine when the room grew quiet. It seemed worse in my bedroom.

My sweet cat, Samantha, began avoiding that room as well, preferring to sleep on the back of the couch in the living room. At first, I blamed it on the constant draft that seemed to linger in the bedroom, despite all attempts to dispel it. The living room was warmer for her, especially when she was stretched out across the back of the couch, soaking up the afternoon sunshine.

"What's the matter, Sammy?" I asked her. She stared back at me with her wide green eyes. If cats could only talk, I'm sure she had much to tell me.

I started paying more attention to her. Something was truly bothering her.

She was always fastidious about using her litter box, but I started finding evidence of her indiscretions in various places in the house. Her favorite place to urinate was the closet in Laura's room, where my husband kept his clothes.

My husband had never been a big fan of cats, professing an allergy to them, something I would always question. His allergies seemed to be selective, if not psychosomatic. Many times, I watched him sit on a couch that was covered with cat hair without exhibiting any symptoms. Other times, he would break into hives after a brief exposure to felines. Truthfully, he wasn't a big fan of cats in general. Her pissing in his closet was practically a death sentence. If she didn't stop, she wouldn't last long in the house.

I switched brands of cat litter and even added another litter box in the basement, but she refused to go down there. Something about the basement bothered her as much as the bedroom. I didn't blame her. Both spaces gave me an unsettled feeling as well.

Sometimes when I sat on the couch with her, she would startle awake. Then, she would turn as if watching something in the hallway, her eyes wide with fright. It was the same expression she used when a stranger came into the house. Normally, she'd scramble down the hallway to hide under the bed until the person left. Only this time, the bedroom was off limits for her, as well. Something in that room scared her more than strangers did.

If it was a clue that something odd was happening, I missed it. I blamed it on typical cat behavior.

It was 1990, long before the paranormal world was accepted. There weren't any ghost shows on television. The only books I could find in the library were old and outdated. The only thing I knew about ghosts was from what I'd learned from the movies. The one that always stuck in my mind was the movie *Poltergeist*.

They know what scares you.

Those five words drifted into my mind frequently and I would remember the scene from the movie that terrified me most. The father was getting ready to go into the bedroom where all hell had broken loose. The psychic warned him to clear his mind because they would be able to read it. Once they did, they would find out what he was afraid of and use it against him. The mere thought horrified me.

What was I afraid of?

It wasn't hard to answer. Something was happening to my daughter.

As soon as the thought flashed into my head, I erased it as quickly as possible by singing a children's song in my head, one that we frequently sang to Laura.

"You are my sunshine, my only sunshine.
You make me happy when skies are grey.
You'll never know dear how much I love you.
Please don't take my sunshine away"

But even that was too close to the truth. Taking my sunshine away was synonymous to taking my Laura away.

They know what scares you.

Pressured by the need for more income, I started working several part time jobs. It was a relief to get out of the house, even if it wasn't something enjoyable. I craved being around people and seeing something besides the interior walls of my house.

Working will be good for me, I told myself.

One of my jobs was delivering the afternoon newspaper. It wasn't a job that utilized any of my talents, but it would bring in some extra income.

The entire route took me two and a half hours from start to finish and I did it with Laura strapped into the backseat in her car seat. I wasn't making enough money to pay for a sitter, so it seemed like a simple solution.

She was usually agreeable in the beginning, falling asleep by the time I was halfway finished with my route.

If I were lucky, she remained sleeping until I finished my route, but more often than not, she woke up when I still had an hour left to go.

I drove down the street, blindly shoving papers into the plastic tubes, mentally swearing at the selfish bastards who insisted that I get out of the car to deliver the paper to their front door. Some of these were understandable, especially when it involved an elderly client, but it wasn't always the case. Our town was in a bedroom community.

Being thirty miles outside of Boston, Westborough was swiftly becoming a popular town for the Boston elite. They could enjoy the benefits of suburban life, but still maintain employment in the city. Richer families began moving in, building larger houses on land that had once been pastoral farmland. While most people were fine with walking to the end of their driveway to retrieve their daily newspaper, some of the population insisted that it be hand-delivered to the door. These were the ones I despised the most.

"Ring the doorbell, dear. If no one comes after a few minutes, just leave it on the wicker bench by the door," I was told.

As I left the car parked in the driveway with my baby fastened inside, I ran up the sidewalk, often defying the special requests. I tossed the paper onto the bench and then rang the doorbell. By the time they answered I was halfway down the driveway, thankful that no one had chosen that moment to steal my car and take my baby.

My husband shook his head at my fears.

"We live in Westborough. It's not like carjackers are hiding around every corner," he told me, always poo-pooing my concerns.

I understood what he was saying and knew he was probably right, but how could I continue to take chances with something so precious? There were carjackers *somewhere* out there in the world. Who was to say they didn't sometimes lurk in the suburbs?

"Then, take the keys out and lock the doors, if you're so worried," he countered.

I sighed. I still didn't like it. It just seemed like taking too many chances.

They know what scares you.

The thought rang in my head so often it nearly became my mantra. Having something so precious made me far too vulnerable. I couldn't find a place where I wasn't afraid. Dangers seemed to lie in wait everywhere. I worried when I was home and I worried when I was away. Was I losing my mind?

My other part time job wasn't much better.

A friend who used to work at my last job with me was trying to open his own pet store. He wanted me to help him start the store.

I liked John, but had a difficult time with his life style. His grandfather was the founder of a popular coffee shop chain in New England. When they sold the corporation, he sold all of his stocks, making him an incredibly wealthy young man. He started out by buying a mansion a mile away from me in one of the fancy neighborhoods. Then, he decided to open a business.

His house often smelled like pot smoke and was filled to the brim with a menagerie of animals. I never knew what was going to great me at the door. Sometimes it would be a German Shepard puppy, other times it might be a Hyacinth Macaw or an iguana. Clothes and trash littered the floor. If the puppy soiled on them, they often went unnoticed. While John and I plotted out his business, I kept Laura firmly on my hip. There was no way I was letting her down to crawl around at that house.

John stopped by my house one day to drop off some paperwork he wanted me to look at.

I invited him in, not even bothering to tell him to excuse the mess. After seeing his house, mine was spotless by comparison. I moved a handful of toys off the couch so he could sit down. As he brushed past me, I caught the distinctive smell of pot clinging to his clothes. He smoked it so often, it wasn't abnormal to smell it on him. I didn't know if he'd just finished a joint or if it had just permeated into his clothing.

I tried not to be judgmental. I smoked my fair share in my youth, but I didn't like the way it left him. He was often flighty and moody. I never knew which John I would encounter.

Laura cooed at him, reaching out with a pudgy arm.

"Hey there, baby," he said, smiling at her. He was surprisingly good with her, always taking the time to acknowledge her. He handed her a toy, then glanced up at the hallway. His face froze in place.

"Oh my God. Did you see that?" he gasped.

I swiveled around, trying to figure out what he was looking at, but it was long gone by the time I turned.

He was still staring at the hallway.

"What did you see?" I asked.

"I swear I just saw a black shadow move from the kitchen down the hallway," he said.

I stood up, shifting Laura to my hip. "What do you mean? What kind of shadow?"

He rose with me, but seemed apprehensive about following me to the hallway. "I swear to God, it looked just like a person. It was like a solid black shadow that was shaped like a man," he said.

His words spiked through me, followed by a rush of fear. I didn't know what to do. Should I walk down the hallway to make sure there wasn't somebody in the house? Or should I grab the cordless phone off the kitchen counter and call the police?

As I stood there indecisively, the cat flew down the hall from the direction of my bedroom. She stopped at the doorway, frozen in fear as she tried to decide what was scarier: the stranger in front of her or what had caused her to bolt out of the bedroom. It was enough to set me into motion.

"I need to go look and make sure somebody isn't in the house," I whispered to him, in case the person could hear me. "Can you hold Laura for a minute? Just stand by the door. If I scream, run outside. Okay?" I asked.

He nodded and took the baby.

I didn't give him time to reconsider. Despite the smell of pot on his clothes, I handed him my daughter and started towards the hallway. Even if he was stoned out of his mind, which I didn't think he was, he was the lesser of the two evils. I grabbed the cordless phone off the counter and handed it to him.

"If I scream, call the police from outside," I whispered.

I took a deep breath to push the fear out of my system and headed down the hallway.

How could somebody be in the house? My mind swirled around the thought, trying to make sense of it. Could it be John's imagination running rampant? I considered the way he smelled as he came through the door. Was the pot making him paranoid?

I wasn't sure what to hope for, but the thought made me move a little faster.

At the end of the hallway were two doorways. One led into Laura's room and the other led to my bedroom. I glanced into Laura's room and was able to see the entire room with one glance. There wasn't anywhere to hide in the sparsely furnished room. The closet doors were shut, but if someone had closed them behind himself, I would have heard the sound of the squeaky door.

That just left my bedroom.

I pushed the door open and looked around the room. Nothing.

I heaved a sigh of relief.

"It's okay. Nobody's here," I said, taking a quick peek in the closet just in case.

I made my way back to the living room and took Laura from his arms. She smiled up at me and babbled something that sounded like "Bob." She'd been saying it lately, turning it into a standing joke between my husband and I, when we were in the mood to laugh.

"Who's Bob?" he'd ask, pretending to be jealous.

"I don't know, but if you find him, let Laura know. She's been looking for him all day," I countered. This time there were no jokes. I believed John saw something. I just wasn't sure what it was. A part of me didn't want to consider that it was the ghost. It was much easier to pretend that it was just a hallucination on John's part.

He left soon afterwards, all conversation about the papers he delivered long forgotten. I had a difficult time getting him to come back after that.

The house was not the happy place I hoped for. It was becoming a torture chamber.

How could I admit that this was happening? Who could I tell? I thought about it for the rest of the afternoon, pondering the options and coming up short. Every person I knew would tell me I was imagining things, even my husband.

He came home hours later, but I kept the information to myself.

I simply waded through the evening, going through the motions, while playing the scene over and over again in my mind. Maybe John was just high. Maybe he saw an odd shadow and made more out of it than it really was.

Then, it would come back around full circle.

What about the cat?

Something startled her, causing her to bolt down the hallway. I couldn't get past that.

My husband headed to bed early, something he normally did each night. I desperately needed some alone time to process everything that happened to me, but I wasn't sure I was up to the challenge of being alone in the house.

I spent ten minutes on the couch before I heard the unmistakable sound of ear ringing.

They know what scares you.

I retreated to bed and curled on my side, willing the sound to evaporate. When sleep finally found me, it wouldn't be the safe haven I prayed for. As soon as I drifted off, the voice came to me.

Come with us.

I screamed until my husband woke me up.

It would soon get much worse.

8

"Want to see my plans for the basement?" my husband asked.

I sighed, feeling a mixture of emotions. I loved daydreaming about the home improvements he wanted to make on the house, but I was also a little worried about our finances. We were barely meeting our bills to begin with, and it didn't make sense to add more expenses to our plate, but it was hard to ignore his excitement.

He wanted to create a family room with a wet bar and a separate room for the washer and dryer. The icing on the cake for me was the built-in fish tank. When he told me that he wanted to create a closet in the space beside the stairs and build an aquarium inside of the wall, it was hard for me to resist.

We kept aquariums for years and always dreamed of having one built into a wall. The one thing that I always hated about aquariums was all the filters and visible equipment. By building it into the wall, we could hide all that, leaving the exterior framed like a painting. It was hard not to get excited.

He walked back upstairs with the plans and left me alone in the basement. As I stood there, cold chills raced up my arms.

Could I really stay down there long enough to clean an aquarium?

Something was wrong about the basement.

I couldn't put my finger on what it was, but it just didn't give me a good feeling. I tried to convince myself that it was just visual. It looked like a creepy basement. Every haunted house horror movie I could remember always featured a scary basement. Maybe I was just projecting my fears.

I looked around, trying to imagine the space transformed into a living room, but I couldn't see it. The walls would definitely have to be repainted. I got another chill just looking at them.

The walls near the fireplace were painted the color of blood. It wasn't the red you often see in trendy kitchens and dining rooms. It was the color that would come out of your veins if you ran a knife across them. It reminded me of satanic worship, of animals sacrificed on a long stone table, their blood splashed against the wall in honor of a dark god.

I later learned that red is the color of protection.

It's the color of the candles that witches use to banish negative energy in their most powerful spells. It is the color psychic mediums often paint their doors to ward off evil entities. It is the color of blood, but it is also the color of fortification. A wall painted red could hold back a world full of evil.

It was apparent the previous owners knew more than I did.

My husband didn't see any of this. He simply saw the opportunity for the unused space.

The red walls would be covered with pure white sheetrock, erasing any memory that had once lingered there. I couldn't be as certain. The thought of those red walls haunted me nearly as much as the sight of the old workbench. The minute he carried it outside and smashed it into pieces, the activity began to escalate.

It was no longer imagined.

It became real in the span of a heartbeat.

<u>9</u>

A year passed since I first sensed something in the house, but it was so subtle I couldn't be certain it was real. I tried to blame it on my imagination because that was far easier to contend with.

Most of the things that happened in the beginning could almost be explained. The only thing I couldn't quite get past was the shadow man John saw in the hallway, coupled with my cat's simultaneous reaction.

When I mentioned the possibility of a haunting to John's girlfriend, she asked me about the power lines that ran across our property. I hadn't given them much thought. When we first moved in, they were initially a concern because I didn't know what kind of impact they would have on our health, and more importantly, on the health of our baby daughter. I was reassured that the house was a safe enough distance from them and that I shouldn't worry. She thought otherwise.

"My father's an electrician. High power lines like that put off a huge amount of electromagnetic energy," she told me.

"What can that do to people?" I asked.

"Well, my dad went to somebody's house. They were having electrical issues in the basement. While they were there, the guy told my dad to be careful in the basement because it was haunted. My dad laughed because he doesn't believe in ghosts, but what he found made a lot of sense. The wiring was all screwed up in the guy's electrical box and it was sending out crazy amounts of electromagnetic energy. My dad says that when people are around that for long periods, it can make them feel like they're being watched or even have hallucinations. They call it a fear cage," she said.

It gave me something to consider. One of the biggest signs I was feeling was the sensation of being watched. Was it from the power lines? Was I being impacted by a fear cage?

If we had the Internet back then, I could have answered the question quickly, but the technology was years away. I tried to look the information up at the library, but the books were dry and difficult to comprehend. If the information I needed was there, it was buried deep in a dusty old book.

I just took what she said to heart.

Maybe it was just my imagination.

I tried to ignore the sensation that someone was watching me, but it just wouldn't go away. I stood at the sink washing dishes and felt someone walk up behind me. The floors squeaked as if from invisible footsteps and I caught a whiff of cigar smoke. I swiveled around only to find myself alone.

How could I be imagining all of that?

I didn't say anything to my husband for a long time. Things were quickly disintegrating between us. I didn't want to add more fuel to the fire. A part of me was afraid he was just going to take my daughter and leave me, telling the courts that I was blue-goose crazy.

The only person I could talk to about it was John, because he saw it with his own eyes, but he was too caught up with his new pet store to have much to offer. It soon became my cross to bear.

I tried to put it into a context that made sense to me. It was as though the old man in the basement was agitated that new people moved into his house. He must have known that his house couldn't remain empty forever. Someone would eventually move in and claim the space. What set him off was the basement remodeling.

I saw him clearly in my mind.

He was an older man who was unhappy with his life, and especially his marriage. His wife was difficult, always nagging, unhappy with everything he did. Every time she saw him, a honey-do list sprang into her mind, starting with the things he still hadn't accomplished from the last list. The basement was the only place he could go to get away from her.

She didn't like the stairs. She said they bothered her knees, which was fine with him.

She would open the door and yell down at him on occasion, but if he just remained silent, she eventually closed the door again and went back to her miserable life. When his workbench was ripped away, it was *her* all over again. She was taking away the only thing in the world that had brought him pleasure.

Damn her.

Blind rage filled his body. He wanted nothing more than to wrap his hands around her throat and squeeze the life from her. Somehow, in his imaginings, *she* became *me.*

I was the target.

I knew this with the same surety that I knew the house was blue. I saw it in my mind, felt it in my soul. Proof would be a little harder to provide since it was just my thoughts. I couldn't produce the man and stand him in front of my husband and say "see?" He was as invisible as the worry that consumed my mind.

And he knew what scared me.

He began to target me when I was alone.

I came home one evening an hour before my husband was due to arrive.

As I pulled into the driveway, something caught my eye. The front door was wide open and the lights in the kitchen were on. I frowned, trying to remember my morning.

I was the last person to leave the house that morning. My friend John had opened his pet store by then and had hired me as his manager. That meant that Laura had to go to daycare. Getting her ready in the mornings was as much fun as trying to catch greased pigs. She didn't want to leave the house. She also didn't want to get dressed, eat breakfast, or have her hair brushed. She was only fourteen months old, but she was already a handful. Still though, I don't think I would have left the front door open. Why would I have opened it in the first place?

I parked the car and just sat there for a moment, listening to the engine tick as it cooled down. We hardly ever used the front door. There was no reason for it to be open. When we left the house, we always used the door in the basement because of the close proximity to our parked cars. We only used the front door when guests came to visit, which was seldom the occurrence.

I unbuckled Laura from her car seat and carried her to the door. I jiggled the doorknob, almost expecting to find it unlocked too, but it was locked tight, like I left it. I slipped my key into the lock and stepped inside, leaving the bitter January winds behind us.

The basement smelled like sawdust, which was a definite improvement over the mold and mildew. My husband had started clearing out the basement. The first thing he did was cart out the old workbench. Pieces of it sat beside the garage in a pile. Inside, the room was empty, save for a pile of new lumber that was pushed against the wall.

I flipped on the light switch, feeling fear climb my spine. I hated being in the basement when it was dark.

Even though the basement was a walkout, with a door and two windows looking out into the back yard, the area was still gloomy. It was almost as though it wanted to be dark, that it pulled the darkness in closer. Even the bulbs on the ceiling barely made a dent. All I could see from the doorway was the stairs and a small portion of the middle of the room. The rest was lost in shadows. I shivered, trying to get ahold of myself.

I carried Laura up the stairs on my hip, listening absently to her chatter all the way up. When we got to the top of the stairs, I stopped at the doorway and looked around for a few seconds, trying to get a grip on my nerves. Nobody was there. I was simply letting my imagination get the better of me.

It's just the power lines, I tried to tell myself.

I closed the front door and parked Laura on the kitchen floor with a handful of toys. She started walking when she was eleven months old, but she liked to hang out with me while I cooked. I pulled the chicken out of the refrigerator and turned towards the oven to begin preheating it when something caught my eye. The front door was wide open again.

I just stood there, frozen in place with the package of raw chicken dangling from my hand.

I could have imagined many things, but I knew I closed that door. I heard the lock click in place. The only way for it to be open was if someone turned the knob and pulled on the door.

As I looked around with wide eyes, my ears began ringing. The sound started out soft, but began growing louder and louder until my head nearly exploded with the noise.

"What do you want?" I asked, feeling foolish at the sound of my voice.

I could feel a sense of anger swirl around me.

Was it real or imagined?

Terror gripped me from the inside out. I wanted to grab my daughter and run back out to my car, like I'd done when I was seventeen years old at my father's house, but I couldn't. I had much more at stake. If I ran, I had nowhere to go. I had to come back eventually with the knowledge that I let an unseen force chase me out.

They know what scares you.

If I showed it the fear that laced through me with icy fingers, then I'd only be opening myself up to more. I took a deep breath and closed my eyes for a moment.

It's going to be okay.

When I opened them, the ringing had softened.

I reached down to turn the oven on, only to find it already switched on to three-hundred and fifty degrees, the temperature I was planning on setting it. I backed away from the oven, nearly tripping over Laura in the process.

In the back of my mind, I could feel him laughing.

The sound rang through me, echoing inside my head like thunder.

What was I going to do?

10

My friend's pet store only made it to the five month mark before he grew disinterested and closed it. That left me in a serious predicament. I needed a job.

I frantically searched the want-ads, not sure about what I wanted.

I already had invested quite a few years into the pet industry, so a retail environment seemed like a good place to start, but management jobs were few and far between. What I really wanted was to open my own store.

I could clearly see it in my head. It would be a mixture of gift shop and pet store. I'd have beautiful hand-crafted gifts hanging side-by-side with vintage bird cages, filled with colorful finches. Fish tanks would burble in the back of the store, stocked with exotic fish from all around the world. People could chose from custom aquariums shaped like coffee tables or globes, or just go with the traditional rectangular version. I would turn the concept of pet stores into something undiscovered.

I began drawing up a business plan. Since I already helped John open his store, I had a list of vendors to contact. I tried to buy my friend's business, but he was asking too much money, and besides, it wasn't in a great location. The rent was far more than a pet store could handle, compared to the traffic that moved past his door.

I began driving around, looking at properties with Laura in the backseat.

It didn't take me long to find the location of my dreams. It was a small space, but it was nestled into the perfect plaza. There was a larger department store at one end, serving as the anchor store, followed by a plethora of small businesses, similar to my own dream store. There was an art supply shop, a card store, a hair salon, a clothing boutique, and many others. I'd fit right in.

I was so excited, I forgot that I didn't have John's options.

Big things only came to those with big money.

When I went to the bank to get a loan, I was promptly turned down. If I wanted the money I needed, I would have to put my house up as collateral, but I couldn't risk it. We didn't have a lot, but what we did have was precious. I couldn't risk losing our house if the business didn't succeed.

It was back to the drawing board.

I was so depressed, I barely drug myself out of bed each morning.

It just didn't seem fair. Why couldn't I have been born into a rich family? John didn't have to worry about a thing. He just drifted from one venture to another. As soon as he closed the business, he also sold his house and moved to Florida to open an exotic bird farm. I couldn't even afford to vacation in Florida, never mind move there and purchase my second business of the year.

I went back to the want-ads and found a part-time job at a pet supply store twenty miles from home. It wasn't what I wanted, but I needed to work. The basement renovation project was costing more than we expected and we needed the money. And besides, Laura really missed going to daycare. She had made several close friends there and was bored with our home routine.

I accepted the job offer and started my job a few days later.

I was hired as a cashier. My job was to stand in front of a cash register and smile, two things I did well. Unfortunately, it was also boring work. I quickly found myself drifting away from the register to straighten shelves or assist customers. They seemed to appreciate my efforts, so it wasn't long before my twenty hours a week turned into forty.

In the meantime, the activity at my house was steadily picking up. The phantom footsteps happened daily and items began disappearing, only to reappear somewhere else.

My husband finally began experiencing some of the ghostly commotion. One night after dinner, he retreated to the basement to work on the remodeling project. Shortly afterwards, I heard him yell at the dog. Curious, I went down to see what was going on.

"Sheba keeps carrying off my tools. First it was my screwdriver and now it's my hammer," he said, glaring at the dog lying on the floor beside him.

Sheba was my husband's dog. There was no doubt about it. She followed him around the house when he was home, preferring to lay on the cold cement floor in the basement with him instead of being upstairs with me.

I looked at Sheba, who wagged the tip of her tail as she peered up with her big brown eyes.

"You really think she can carry a hammer?" I asked.

He was measuring wood with a tape measure, putting marks on it so he knew where to cut it when he brought it to the table saw. He barely brushed me with a glance as he moved to the table.

He'd been spending more and more time in the basement working. Sometimes I wondered if he was just doing it to avoid me. We were quickly growing further apart, something that bothered me greatly now that we had a child together. I didn't want Laura to grow up with divorced parents like I had endured, but I was also tired of always feeling as though I got the short end of the stick. Instead of helping me with the baby, he came home and immediately went down to the basement on the pretense of working.

"How else would the hammer end up across the room?" he asked, then turned on the saw, drowning out any possibility of hearing my reply.

I waited until he was finished, something I was getting used to. It seemed like the longer we were in the house, the fewer nice things we did for one another.

There was a time when my question would have warranted his attention, but it was clear that cutting the wood was a higher priority for him. It made me sad.

We used to take off for the weekend and explore New England. Sometimes, we would set up a tent in the middle of a national park for an impromptu adventure. Now that we had responsibilities, like a child and a house to care for, we no longer did those things.

I took a deep breath.

"I think our house is haunted," I said, then waited for his reaction, hoping he'd listen to me.

He cut another piece of wood and then turned to regard me.

"Haunted?" he asked.

I could almost see the ghost in the basement tossing thoughts his way.

They played across his face one by one.

She's beginning to lose it.

I misplace a screwdriver and she blames it on ghosts?

"Other things have happened. When I came home from work the other day, the front door was open and the lights were on," I started, but he didn't give me a chance to finish.

"That door doesn't close right. If you don't latch it tight, it pops back open," he said and then dismissed me.

I would have gone on to tell him about John's experience and the way the cat was acting, but it as clear he wasn't going to change his mind.

If a wall was being built between us, I stacked another brick on it before making my way upstairs to deal with my terror alone.

Laura had recently moved from her crib into a bed that we referred to as her big girl bed. I purchased sheets decorated with characters from her favorite movies, hoping to lure her back into the bed. The only problem with a big girl bed was the fact that she could climb out of it anytime she wanted. There would be no more putting her to bed with the knowledge she'd remain there. She popped back up minutes later, wanting a drink of water, a cookie,or more books to be read to her.

After three books, which was the agreed upon amount, I finally turned off the light and closed her door. My mind was screaming for free time, but my body craved a bath. I decided to combine the two and bring a book into the bathroom, where I'd read it while soaking in a tub full of bubbles.

As soon as I turned the water on, I heard a strange sound.

It almost sounded like a baby crying.

I turned it off and listened, but couldn't hear the sound any longer. I turned it back on and the baby crying came back.

"This is strange," I mumbled to myself. I left the water running and walked down the hallway to press my ear against Laura's door. It was as quiet as it was when I left her. I walked to the basement door and cracked it open an inch. My husband was still in the basement sawing wood. Nothing he was doing sounded anything like babies crying. I sighed.

Maybe it was just my imagination.

I returned to the bathroom to discover another surprise.

The water had been turned off and the drain was unplugged. All my precious bubble bath water had drained down the pipes, leaving me with an empty tub. A normal person would have just given up, but I wasn't so easily persuaded. I didn't care what the ghost thought. I needed a bath.

I ran the water again and sat on the side of the tub until it was full.

As I slipped into the soapy hot water, I grew uncomfortable as I wondered if someone was watching me. How could I continue living like this?

Unfortunately, what had happened was nothing compared to what was coming.

(Above) Laura with Sheba and Buddy

11

Laura was just under two years old when I brought her to Indiana to see my family. Visiting my family was always a happy time for me. I missed my home state more than I thought I would. Moving to the other side of the country had left a tremendous hole in my life. *Joni moved to the moon,* my father would say with a sigh. It felt like the moon. Nothing was familiar and the environment was often harsh and unforgiving.

I always thought that when I had children, I'd be surrounded by friends and family who would share in my joy and help me when I needed assistance, but motherhood had been nothing like that for me. I felt almost as though I had been stranded on another world, void of friends and other people. My in-laws were wonderful people, but they lived over an hour away from us. We usually only saw them on holidays or group birthday events.

Since adolescence, I was slow in making friends. I simply felt socially awkward around other people. I never knew what to say to them, and I hated making a fool of myself. The town we settled in was filled with people I didn't understand. The fathers worked all day and the mothers were super moms, the kind of women who scheduled play dates and took frequent outings to the local museums for fun.

I wasn't that kind of person. I always got along better with men than I did with other women. I didn't understand their joy behind things like fashion and home decorating. Trends were something I couldn't afford, even if I'd wanted to. I was more of a loner, but it was starting to affect me. I needed to see people who understood me, and I wasn't finding that in my new town.

Laura and I ended up taking the trip to Indiana alone. My husband wanted to stay home to finish the basement project. I didn't argue with him, even though it would have been nice to get away as a family. I was finding that we were doing less and less together. In the evenings, he went directly downstairs after dinner to work on the basement. The space was beginning to feel like the other woman to me. I couldn't wait until it was finished and I could have my husband back again.

The trip to Indiana was a blur of faces. I tried to budget my time, spending equal parts with my father and step-mother at the A-frame, and with my mother and step-father at their house, but I always felt like I was short changing someone. My trips back were wonderful, but exhausting, leaving me feeling like I needed a vacation to recover from my vacation.

One thing was for certain though, I was happy to find someone to share my stories with. I found my confidante in my younger sister, Leah.

Being five years younger than me, she was the one person who believed my stories about the ghost in the house. When everybody else rolled their eyes and praised me for my excellent imagination, Leah listened to me with wide eyes, never doubting that what I was telling her was the truth.

Part of the reason for our trip back was to attend her college graduation. I was so proud of her for the accomplishment. It was something I hadn't been able to achieve, but I was happy she made it through nonetheless. It hadn't been easy for her. She worked several part-time jobs trying to support herself while taking a full load of classes. Now that she graduated, she'd be able to find a job in her field of psychology.

I pulled her aside the first chance I got and told her about some of the things that had been happening. Since my bathtub incident, where I heard the baby crying, the activity had become steady. I frequently came home to find the doors open and the lights on. Footsteps at the other end of the house were so frequent, I barely looked up anymore when I heard them.

"What should I do?" I asked her.

"Can you just sell the house and move?" she asked. It was the logical answer, but unfortunately it wouldn't work.

"It's only been happening when I'm around," I said.

I didn't want to tell her that my husband didn't believe me, but she seemed to understand regardless. She shook her head, not having any other suggestions. If nothing else, it was a relief to share it with someone who fully believed me.

As things continued to happen, I stopped bringing them up. It was clear that he needed to experience some of the paranormal activity before he could get a firm grip on what was happening. It wasn't so much that he didn't believe me, it was more that he hadn't seen it first-hand. I could almost understand his earlier reaction. While he hadn't outright said that it was just my imagination, I was fairly certain that was what he thought. It would take something monumental before he came around.

As it turns out, that event happened the day I returned home from my Indiana trip.

He picked us up at the airport, telling us that he had a surprise for us when we got home.

Laura was so excited to see her daddy, she talked to him the entire way home, telling him about her potty training experience.

Typical of my tenacious daughter, she decided to begin her long awaited potty training in route to Indiana. This meant frequent stops at the airport restrooms and twice on the plane. I think the novelty of the different bathrooms was a major draw to my young explorer, but true to form, she was almost fully potty trained by the time we arrived back home. Once she made her mind up to do something, nothing would stop her.

We pulled up at the house and he made us wait outside the door to the basement while he went in and turned on all the lights.

I held Laura's hand tightly, eager to see what he was going to show us. In my heart, I really hoped that the basement project was finally finished. As a family, were suffering from the impact of the remodel project. The distance that had grown between us was getting deeper and deeper. I was afraid that if something didn't bridge the gap, we'd soon find ourselves living in completely different worlds.

"Okay," he said, holding the door open. "Come on in and see it."

We stepped in and stopped, mesmerized by the difference. Instead of the cobweb crusted rafters, the ceiling was covered with sheetrock. The red walls were painted a soothing aquamarine color. Laura was quick to test out the new grey carpeting. She ran to the middle of the room and did an impromptu somersault, then rolled around in glee.

"Check out your fish tank," he said, pointing to the end of the bar where the fish tank was built into the wall.

It was everything I'd ever dreamed of. It was so perfect. It wasn't a huge tank, but it was big enough for the space. I walked over to it, admiring the woodwork around the white paneling. It was like a framed painting. I couldn't wait to fill it with water and fish.

"Walk into the closet and check it out from the inside. You should have plenty of space to maintain it," he said.

I opened the door to the closet. It was larger than most closets. Most people would have used it for storage, but we planned to use it for the dogs. Neither of them were trustworthy in the house alone while we were gone, so they needed to be confined in a safe space where they couldn't get into trouble. Previously, we'd locked them in a metal crate that was barely big enough for the two of them to turn around and lie down comfortably, but this would suit their needs perfectly. It was large enough for a few doggie beds and toys, but not large enough for them to use it as a bathroom as well.

"It's perfect," I said, smiling.

As I stood there, taking it all in, something caught my eye.

The wall inside the closet wasn't finished. You could see the studs and the backside of the paneling. Centered between two of the studs to the left of the fish tank were words. They'd been written in chalk.

I'm here woman.

I gasped when I saw it.

"Did you write that?" I asked.

"Write what?" He came into the closet and looked to where I was pointing. "I'm here woman," he read it aloud. He was quiet for a moment as he searched his memory banks for a logical explanation. "I have no idea how that got there. Nobody was here except for me all weekend," he said.

"Who wrote it then?" I asked, a sick feeling creep into the pit of my stomach. I just stared at him, knowing the answer, but not feeling as though I could share it with him.

"Maybe it was your ghost," he said quietly.

Before I could stop him, he reached out and erased part of the writing. "Let's see if it comes back," he said.

He took Laura in his arms and headed upstairs.

I just stood there, long after they left, staring at the writing on the wall, wondering about a lot of things. The message was obviously left there for me.

I'm here woman.

It was the beginning of the end for a lot of things.

I'd never again be happy in that house.

(Above) The aquarium built beneath the stairs

12

I was only at my new job for six months before I was offered a promotion. They wanted me to go to a new store in nearby Shrewsbury, where I would act as the assistant manager. I was ecstatic. Shrewsbury was much closer to me than the other store. It would cut my commute in half. Another added bonus was that the promotion came with a pay raise.

At first, it was a dream come true. I was back to managing. I looked forward to the challenge of taking something good and making it better. I loved working with people and helping to mold them into productive members of a team. Unfortunately, it would pull me away from home for long hours at a time and would eventually alter my life in ways I didn't plan on.

The paranormal activity at home continued along the same path. There was almost never a day that I didn't drive up to the house and discover a door open or a light turned on that I had turned off before leaving. It came to a point where it didn't scare me anymore. As soon as I came to expect it, he would add something new.

I was already late for work one morning when I couldn't find my keys.

I pulled on my coat, and got Laura bundled up before grabbing my purse. I reached in, expecting to find my keys, but they weren't there.

"Damn it," I swore under my breath.

I have always been meticulous about my habits and I hate looking for things. My house wasn't the cleanest, but it was organized. I assigned homes for nearly every item in my house, especially those that I needed quickly. I might have let the kitchen floor go a few days before washing it, but I was diligent about putting things back after I used them. It just made it easier to locate things when I needed them.

With a toddler in the house, it was normal to have items moved around, so it took me a while to figure out what was really happening. I didn't even bother to grill Laura about my keys, though. I knew where I put them and they weren't there. Since my purse was hung on a high hook in a closet, I knew she hadn't taken them.

I dug around a little more with my free hand before giving up and putting Laura on the floor, so I could dump the purse upside down on the kitchen table. I even turned the lining inside out, but the keys weren't there.

"Son of a...," I started, stopping myself short of another swear. With Laura picking up new words and phrases by the minute, the last thing I wanted was for her to go to daycare and start telling everyone they were bitches. I stopped for a minute and closed my eyes, trying to retrace my last steps.

I came home from work the previous night at six. I hadn't gone grocery shopping or stopped anywhere along the way home. Laura's aunt Audra picked her up at daycare, so I didn't even have that distraction to factor in. I shoved my hand in my coat pocket, hoping to find them there, but my pockets were full of tissues, gloves, and a sticky lollipop Laura had handed me. No keys.

With a sigh, I checked the clock. I was now officially late. There was no way I would make it there on time. The employees would be standing out in the cold, waiting for me to open the door. In fifteen minutes, they would be joined by customers who wanted inside the store. If I wasn't there, someone would call the corporate office and I was sure to get chewed out.

I began a quick search of the house, doing a sweep through each room before going back and looking at them more carefully. I even ran out to the car to see if they were in the ignition, but didn't find them. I ended up finding them in the refrigerator in the produce drawer.

"Seriously. You have to stop doing this to me," I whispered.

I hadn't opened the produce drawer in days, which was evident by the soggy head of lettuce that was leaking putrid juices on the bottom of the drawer. I grab the keys and headed out, wondering what excuse I was going to use when I got to work. A story about a ghost hiding my keys just wouldn't cut it.

I was a bit dismayed that my husband still had not experienced anything beyond the writing on the wall. It was becoming harder and harder to deal with these issues on my own. It was as though Gus was targeting me, deliberately leaving him out of the loop. That would change quickly in one night.

I often covered evening shifts, closing the store at nine and then making my way home after all the completing all the paperwork and the neatening the store. One night when I came home, my husband gave me a curious expression. He rose from the couch in the basement as I came through the door.

"Did you just come in the kitchen door upstairs?" he asked.

I was a little dumbfounded by the question. It was snowing outside and the last thing I would have done was park the car on the street, walk up the unshoveled sidewalk to come in through the kitchen door, only to go back out and pull into my normal spot by the basement door.

"No. Why?" I asked.

The look of perplexity swiftly changed to panic. "Because someone just came in through the kitchen door few minutes ago and walked across the kitchen floor. I heard the door close, and then I footsteps," he said.

We raced upstairs thinking the worst. Our daughter was sleeping in her bedroom and someone might be upstairs with her. My husband made it up first. He glanced towards the kitchen at the closed door before heading directly to Laura's bedroom. I came up behind him and peered over his shoulder. Laura was sleeping peacefully, her mouth slack from sleep.

"Check our bedroom?" I asked, not wanting to be the first one in there in case there was an actual person. My heart pounded as he opened the door and walked into our bedroom. A quick inspection was all it took to see that the room was empty.

"Nobody's there," he said.

In my mind, I knew what it was, but it frightened me that he had been able to do something so physical. If he could open and close doors, what would stop him from pulling us out of bed by our ankles or planting butcher knives in our backs while we slept?

They know what scares you.

I quickly erased my mind with the Sunshine song. There was no need to give him ideas that he might not have thought of before.

We exchanged long glances.

At bedtime the night before, Laura usually chose the same three books each night. They were all Disney books, involving a princess, a mermaid, and a fawn, and we knew them by heart after reading them so many times. This night, though, she chose something different.

"I want the Gus is a ghost book," she said.

Her request froze me to the spot. As much as I wanted to ask her why, I held back. I wasn't sure I wanted to know. It was easier to convince myself there was another explanation. Maybe it had fallen out of the bookcase and she noticed it for the first time.

But why would it fall out of the bookcase?

I shook my head, trying to dismiss the thought. Maybe it was better getting the truth. My imagination was probably far worse than any reality.

"Do they read this at daycare?" I asked, praying she'd say yes.

"No. I just wanna hear it," she said.

I read the book, feeling a chill lodge itself somewhere at the base of my spine the entire time I was reading it. I wanted to ask her more questions, but I also didn't want to scare either. I just read the book as quickly as possible, well aware that our invisible housemate was probably also listening. I couldn't remember much about the book, but prayed it didn't end up with a mass murder or anything even remotely close. Thankfully it didn't. Of course, it was a children's book. What had I expected?

"She asked me to read her the Gus is a Friendly Ghost book tonight," I told my husband.

He stared at me, as if weighing the possibilities.

He could no longer dismiss my notions now that he had also witnessed some of Gus's shenanigans. I could nearly see the logical side of his brain spinning, trying to come up with a reasonable explanation.

"I want to check the back door. If someone came in, there will be footprints in the snow," he said instead. We walked across the kitchen floor to the back door.

The floor was dry. If someone had walked in from outside, there would have been snowy footprints on the floor, but there weren't. Outside was the same story. The snow was unmarked.

I could have turned it back around at him, asking him if he was positive he heard footsteps on the floor, suggesting it was just his imagination. I turned the words over in my mind, finding some satisfaction in the thought. Instead, I just shrugged my shoulders.

"Well, I guess if nothing else, we now have a name for our ghost," I said, not feeling any better about the situation. Giving him a name made him real, something that made my stomach clinch.

Gus would continue to up the ante every chance he got.

Eventually he would drive us from the property, but he still had a lot up his sleeve before he was ready to do that.

(Above) Laura and Joni in happier times

13

1993 would be a trying year for me. My life changed in ways I could have never imagined.

In the outside world, life was changing as well. Bill Clinton became our new president, the World Trade Center in Manhattan was bombed, police endured a bloody standoff in Waco, Texas, and twelve year-old Holly Piiranian was abducted from nearby Grafton. Michael Jackson was facing child molestation charges, Prince Charles and Lady Diana separated, and River Phoenix died of a drug overdose outside a New York City nightclub. It was also the year of Jurassic Park, the grunge look, and *Father Figure*, by George Michael.

In my world, I was finally coming into my own.

After a childhood full of apprehension, I finally found the courage to be myself. In the past, I always clung to people, allowing them to determine my direction in the world, but my new job forced me to become a leader.

I began making decisions and delegating tasks to others so we could complete a larger body of work in a shorter amount of time. I matched people to the tasks that suited them, giving them a sense of the same confidence that I was enjoying. We worked as a team, reaping the praise as a unified group, pushing harder to make it even better. We took real pride in what we did. Our store was the best in the chain. Our sales were high and the aisles were neatly stocked.

I put away my craft paints and my crocheting projects and began spending my off-hours socializing with my friends from work. Several nights a week, I followed them to local bars and pool halls, where we spent half the night drinking and laughing. While I knew it wasn't the right thing for a married woman to do, I was helpless to resist it. I never had that before.

I met my husband when I was eighteen years-old and fearful of the world. The strength and bravery that initially attracted me to him became something I allowed to mold my own life. He parted the crowds for me, providing me with safe passage and I clung to his arm, wide-eyed and thankful. By my twenty-first birthday, we were already ensconced in a domestic situation, playing house and allowing our lives to become solid and steady. The following year we married and moved far from my home state. Coming into my own wasn't something that either of us anticipated.

I became fearless and strong, wanting things that were of my making, not those handed to me. I protested against the confines of the walls around me. I wanted more and I became shameless in my desire to push my boundaries.

At first, my husband tolerated it, probably thinking that it was just a stage that I would grow out of, but when it didn't, he became angry and vocal. He did not like me going out without him, but he did not want to go with us either. He wanted to continue staying at home, playing grown-up, something that made me feel weary and old.

I was tired of all the responsibilities. All I ever did was work, and then take care of our house and our child. I spent most of my life doing what I was told, like the good girl that I was. Now, everything was different. I began to wonder what it would be like to be single, making my own rules for a change. It was the ultimate act of rebellion.

At first, it was deliciously alluring. I was able to cast off all the spirit-crushing duties and just have fun. I dressed in pretty clothes, taking pride in my appearance for the first time in my life, and enjoyed the attention it garnered me. People wanted to be around me. They didn't give me disappointed looks or berate me for every little thing I did wrong. They just liked being with me.

They sought me out at the end of our shift to tell me of their plans.

A new band was playing in Worcester?

Count me in.

Playing billiards at Boston Billiards?

Yes, please.

The once- in-a-while excursions quickly turned into several nights a week. I was drunk on the attention and frivolity of simply having fun. We went wherever we wanted and stayed as late as we could. We drank, danced, and laughed. For the first time in my life, I felt like I was a part of something truly special, something that only happened once in a lifetime. After a childhood of not fitting in, I was exhilarated to be one of the master players.

I knew I was pushing my luck with my husband, and in some ways, I probably did it on purpose. I was tired of being oppressed, criticized, and held to his unwavering standards. I began to form my own opinions and make my own rules. When he packed his bags and left, I was surprised, but not shocked.

The first trial separation only lasted twenty-four hours, but was followed by two more over the course of a summer. He left the first two times and I left the last time, renting an apartment for a month in the town where I worked.

It was a relief to be away from the house and away from the haunting, but it was also painful too. All of the constants were stripped away. Gone was my couch by the window, where I sat daydreaming, and my sunny kitchen where I baked bread and washed dishes while watching Laura play in the yard outside. In its place was a small, sterile apartment that felt smaller than it actually was. The parties soon became brash and meaningless. The friends became shallow and predictable.

After the first two weeks, I began to wonder if this was truly what I wanted.

I wanted freedom, but I also wanted stability.

I wanted a nice roof over my head, but I wasn't willing to give up my confidence and willfulness to have it. I also hated what the separation was doing to my daughter. She was carted from one home to another without any constants in her life. I couldn't provide her with all the comforts of home in my tiny apartment and we spent a lot of quiet nights just playing games and watching television. I came to realize what an empty life it would be if I chose it.

By the end of the summer, I made my decision and moved back home. My husband and I started counselling and tried to work things out. For our September anniversary, he surprised me by taking me to Boston for a dinner cruise in Boston Harbor. Steadily, our relationship went back to some sense of normal.

The ghost left me alone for the most part that year. I would still find lights on or doors opened when I came home, but I seldom got the sensation of being watched any longer. My thoughts again turned towards my writing.

I hadn't written anything in years.

My dusty word processor sat abandoned on my desk in the basement, and I looked longingly at it from time to time, willing the words to come to me again.

"You should just try to write something. Sit there until you've gotten at least a few words on the screen," my husband encouraged me.

I gave it some serious thought. Laura was becoming more and more self-reliant and didn't need me as much as she did before. I no longer had any desire to pick up my crafts or crocheting again but I needed something to fill up my creative urges. Since I was no longer drinking them away in bars, I needed to find something to fill the gap in my life.

I carried a mug of coffee to my desk, hopeful that I could pull it off. In my youth, I wrote several short stories, but I was anxious to start a novel. I imagined holding in in my hands, feeling the weight of the paper between the covers. I could almost see it sitting on a bookcase in a bookstore, the spine reading *Joni Mayhan* as though it had always been there, as if it deserved to be there. I began thinking about a story that had been in the back burner of my mind for years and began putting it on paper.

I wanted to write a horror novel, something I should have known better to tackle considering where we lived, but it was my preferred genre. I grew up reading Stephen King and John Saul. I liked the way suspense novels triggered such strong emotions in people. I imagined them reading my books with whitened knuckles, the slightest sound in the dark house making them jolt.

My book was about a veterinarian who was stalked by a serial killer. He tormented her by abducting and maiming her client's dogs, branding them with a strange symbol that she didn't understand. I sat up late after everyone else had gone to bed and wrote. The pages began piling up. I was onto something good.

As soon as I finished a chapter, I saved it on a small disk that was unique to my word processer. Laptops and desktop computers were far too expensive for us to afford, so I just made do with what I had. I showed my printed copies to my husband, who read them, but seldom commented.

"I'm really not a reader," he told me, handing them back.

I got to a point where I just stopped showing them to him. What I needed was a group of people who shared my passion, but I didn't know anyone who wrote, so I just kept it to myself.

One night, we were heading out to have dinner at his mother's house. Before we left, I wanted to make a few changes to a section that I'd been thinking about. I knew I placed the grey disk on the bar in the basement, but couldn't find it.

"Have you seen my disk?" I asked my husband.

"Yeah. It was on the bar earlier today," he said, joining me there to help me look for it.

Since the bar was too tall for Laura to reach, we ruled out the possibility that she might have moved it. We removed everything from the granite laminate bar and determined that it wasn't there. Thoughts of the ghost lingered in the back of my mind, but I pushed them away. He hadn't done anything in a long time. Maybe he was finally getting used to us.

"We need to leave or we're going to be late," he told me.

With reluctance, I followed him out the door, worried that my book was lost forever.

We spent the next few hours with his family and returned later that night. Thoughts of my disk weighed heavily on my mind. If I didn't find it, I would lose all of my work, except for what I had printed out on paper. I really needed to find it.

I walked back to the bar and gasped at what I saw.

The disk was sitting right where I had left it.

Gus was back.

14

The year Laura turned four, we undertook another major construction project. We stripped the house down to a square box and then added a second floor to it.

My husband found a contractor who was willing to do the outside work, leaving the interior details to us. It would save us a tremendous amount of money, but would take years to complete instead of months. I wasn't crazy about the idea to begin with. It seemed like every time we almost caught up with our bills, we added something else to it, but my husband assured me that we could handle it.

It was a nice thought, though. The house was small for three people, especially now that Laura was more active. Having an upstairs would mean that her current bedroom could be repurposed into a toy room and our old bedroom could become my home office for writing.

We should have known that Gus wouldn't like it.

He showed us his displeasure after we tore apart his beloved basement. Pulling the roof of his house would leave him in a combustible rage.

It started with dreams.

Once again, my nights were enveloped with torment. Faceless men chased me down dark alleyways. I woke up just as the knife was descending, my screams waking everyone in the house. I started walking in my sleep again, finding myself bolting down the hallway as if being chased by an unseen demon. I woke with the residue of terror filling my body with panic.

I began feeling him again, lurking in the corners of the room.

He surrounded me with a cloud of anger and hostility, leaving me jumpy and edgy.

I lay awake at night, staring at the doorway, watching the rectangle of light, praying that nothing materialized in the space. The last thing I wanted to do was to see him.

I prayed that he remained hidden in the shadows.

They know what scares you.

I tried to erase the thought from my mind before he could grab onto it, but it was too late.

The edges of the doorway darkened, taking the form of a misty shadow. The overwhelming rush of fear washed over me, riveting me to the bed. I tried to nudge my husband, who slept soundly beside me, but I couldn't move a muscle.

"Just go away," I whispered, the words feeling weak and powerless.

I could feel his anger growling, swirling around him like a vortex. It deepened and darkened, slowly transforming into the shape of a man. He moved closer to me, blocking out the pale light in the hallway.

I pressed my eyes shut and began reciting the Lord's Prayer.

Our father who art in Heaven, hallowed be thy name.

Your God can't save you.

Come with us.

I found myself back on the ski lift with voices in my ears. Was this the same man from my father's house or a new one? Or was Gus using the dream to touch on my deepest fears? I dug my fingers into the covers, pulling them up over my head, as if hiding from the entity in the doorway. After a while, the sensation lessened and the room became normal again.

I somehow found my way to sleep, waking at the edge of dawn to the sound of hammering on the ceiling above me, my mind spinning with the ramifications. It was too late to stop the alterations on the house. The roof and siding were gone. The second floor would be built the following week.

I walked to the sofa in the living room.

If I was a stronger person after my summer unrest, I no longer felt it. I wanted to hide behind someone bigger and stronger so they could shield me from the terror, but there was no one who could help. My husband believed in the haunting after hearing the footsteps in the kitchen, but there wasn't anything he could do to protect me from an invisible monster.

It would be my battle to fight.

I just prayed I had the strength to get through it.

Several days into the project, I found myself on the front step with a few minutes to myself.

After a two-year stint in Shrewsbury, I finally got my own store. They sent me to Dedham, a place the employees referred to as Rat Central.

The old manager was fired at noon on a Monday in January, and they brought me in a half hour later. I knew I was coming into a bad situation, but I had no idea how terrible it would be until I started walking the aisles.

Most of the shelves were empty. Those that weren't bare were stocked with product that had been chewed on by rodents. The first thing I had to do was to get the rodent problem under control. Next would be the employees.

They had been allowed to do what they wanted for several years. Everyone took their dinner break on the carpeted stairs leading to my office, often leaving Taco Bell and McDonald's wrappers and soda cups wherever they last set them. Nobody punched out for breaks and it was common to open the store with only one diligent employee, the rest arriving when they felt like climbing out of bed.

"I know it's a big job, but we want to see what you can do with it," one of the owners told me.

I complied by spending nearly every waking hour there, tearing down shelving, cleaning years of dust and decay away, before putting it back neatly.

I got rid of every rat and employed a team of exterminators to return on a weekly basis to insure none of them returned. I introduced the employees to our policies and procedures, replacing many of them with new people who were more eager to work. I moved entire aisles, gutted the office area and repainted it a pale pink. I trained the staff and taught them how to sell. After sixty hours of work, I was so exhausted, I made myself sick.

I was running a fever. I could feel it dragging my body down, making me lethargic and sweaty. I wanted nothing more than to climb back in bed and fall into a deep sleep where my dreams couldn't touch me, but I couldn't. I was scheduled to work at 1pm.

As I was rising from the steps, stubbing out my cigarette with the tip of my shoe, I saw a truck pull to a stop in front of the house. I recognized the truck right away.

The end of our street turned into a dirt road, before looping towards Southborough and becoming paved again. That left about a half mile of rutted road, which was little more than a path. Joggers and dog walkers used it more than cars. They all gave a wide berth to the shantytown at the edge of the loop though.

The unsavory development must have started with an old house on a large lot. After the house was abandoned, it began decaying into the ground., providing a hidden fortress for squatters.

My husband and I walked back there a few times, picking through the old house, amazed that someone hadn't torn it down to build something else on the spot. The land was prime real estate in a town that was overflowing with new residents. We later found out that an elderly man who lived in Boston was holding the land in trust. He wouldn't allow the land to be sold until after his death, which didn't look like it would happen soon. He was still going strong at 90 years old.

He gave a distant relative permission to tow a camper onto the property, which turned into four campers over a period of five years. We could sometimes hear their music drifting down the street as they sat around a campfire drinking. I used to walk past the area several times a week in my attempt to stay thin and I was always amazed at the collection of old cars and campers.

A clothesline hung between two of the campers, with a dirty blanket draped over it for privacy. In the middle of the opening, someone had chained a calf to a tree.

Mongrel dogs would race out into the road, barking and showing their teeth until someone called them back. It wasn't a great place for a woman alone to walk, so I eventually altered my route to avoid it. The pickup truck that pulled up to my yard belonged to the shantytown. I remembered seeing it parked by the campers.

I paused with one hand on the door handle. Laura was inside playing and my husband was at work. I didn't want the man in my yard, but I wasn't sure what else to do. I could have been rude and raced inside, slamming the door behind me, but I just couldn't do it.

He climbed out of the truck and lumbered around the bumper.

"Can I help you?" I asked, reaching into my pocket for another cigarette.

He waited until he made it to my front porch before he spoke, giving me a chance to look him over better.

He could have been anywhere from fifty to seventy. His long white hair and beard hid most of his face. He was dressed in overalls that were hanging by one shoulder. Beneath it was a tattered greying thermal undershirt. He could have come right off of a movie set about redneck ax murderers. The only thing missing was the ax.

"I just wanted to introduce myself. I used to know the people who lived in your house before," he said.

I sucked in my breath, nearly choking on the cigarette smoke. Maybe he knew about Gus, I thought.

My ears began ringing softly, as though Gus had come out onto the porch to get a look at the man.

"After Bob died, his wife Linda stopped taking care of herself. I used to stop by and bring her food, but they eventually had to move her to a nursing home. It was pretty bad there for a while. She was slinging food against the wall and screaming so loud the neighbors could hear her," he said.

This was interesting information. I didn't know anything about the former owners beyond the man we purchased the house from. Knowing some of the history made it more real to me. Gus might have an actual name.

"Did her husband die in the house?" I asked, almost afraid to hear the answer.

"Yeah. I think he had a heart attack. He was one of those guys who worked himself to death," the man said.

I thanked him for his information and scurried back into the house, needing to get ready to head back into work. I spent the rest of the day thinking about what the old man had told me. It was a lot to consider. I just wasn't sure what to do with it.

The one thing that stuck in my head was the name Bob. It was one of Laura's first words.

15

As soon as we began construction on the house again, a series of events began, bringing us doses of bad luck upon bad luck. Once the progression started, it was like a row of dominoes tipping over onto each other until there was nothing left to fall.

It started innocently enough with a broken dishwasher.

I turned it on, but nothing happened. I told my husband about it when he got home. He looked it over and concluded that the motor had died. Getting a new motor would be costlier than just purchasing a new dishwasher. He promised to take me dishwasher shopping that weekend, but in the meantime, we'd be forced to wash dishes by hand.

That meant I had to pull all the dirty dishes out of the dishwasher that had been fermenting inside of it for days and then wash them in the sink. As I was halfway through the process, wrinkling my nose at the smell, Laura screamed from the bathroom.

I dropped the dish I was washing back into the soapy water and raced into the bathroom, my mind spinning.

Laura was in the bathroom playing with her pet rat, Jasmine. I had no idea what could have happened in the bathroom, but my imagination went into overdrive.

She was bored, so I let her bring Jasmine out for some playtime. We purchased the rat as a pet for Laura several months ago at a local pet store, since the one I worked for didn't sell pets. She initially wanted a hamster, but contrary to popular belief, they don't always make the best pets. They have a tendency to bite and spend all night running on their wheels, which makes them a difficult bedroom pet for a young child. We opted for a baby rat, knowing how sweet and intelligent they were.

While Jasmine was sweet natured, never coming close to biting Laura, she was somewhat of an explorer. If she got down on the ground, she would race across the room, often going into places where she wasn't easily retrieved, like under a bed or couch. We decided to make it easier and let Laura play with her in the empty bathtub where she couldn't get away. The two of them were in the bathroom for almost fifteen minutes before the screaming started.

I rushed in to find blood splashed everywhere. It was all over Laura and all over the white porcelain bathtub.

My heart lunged into my throat as I searched Laura for wounds.

"What happened?" I asked.

She handed me something that was wet with blood. It took me a minute to figure it out and when I did, I dropped it with a shriek. I looked at Jasmine, who was screaming in pain, racing around the bathtub dragging a bloody stump behind her. Somehow, Laura had pulled off the end of her tail.

"Oh my God," I gasped.

I got Laura dressed and loaded the rat up in a pet carrier filled with towels and raced off to the vet.

Over a hundred dollars later, the rat's tail was amputated, and medicated to prevent infection.

Maybe a rat wasn't such a good idea as a pet.

I couldn't figure out how my daughter had managed to pull the animal's tail off. It wasn't like a rat's tail was precariously fastened on. It was part of her body. The best the vet could figure, Laura had grabbed the end of her tail with her fingernails, causing the tail to peel away in her hand.

I came home to clean up the bloody mess with only a few minutes left over to get ready for work.

I looked at the pile of dishes in the sink with a sigh.

I would surely get another dirty look when my husband came home from work and saw them.

What did you do all day?

In retrospect, I probably should have done the dishes and left the bloody mess. Then I could have shown him instead of feeling as though I was just making excuses. I never knew how he was going to react.

Sometimes I wondered if the ghost in the house was getting to him in a different way than it was getting to me. He would wake up some mornings and I knew something was wrong. He carried the blackness with him all day, as if he was lost beneath it. It was like living with two different people some time. One was the husband I knew and loved, but the other was a combustible man who said very little with his mouth, but made up for it with his glare.

Then the next day, everything would be fine.

I walked on eggshells most of the time. I would let him go for two or three days before I asked him what was wrong, because he wouldn't tell me unless I asked. Then by the weekend, all was well. We would have a wonderful time, exploring the northeast.

We purchased a small pop-up camper and began taking family trips together. Some weekends we took the camper to a nearby campground and other times we just jumped in the car and drove wherever we wanted.

Now that Laura was older, we could do those things again. We had even talked about having a second child, but I wasn't sure I was up for it. Could I really go back to a baby who was up all night? Could I really change diapers for two or three years again? On top of it, I wasn't sure we could afford another child. We were barely getting by on our two paychecks. If I quit working, we would lose my paycheck. If I continued working, I would hand the bulk of it over to the daycare providers. Having an infant in daycare was not cheap, even by 1990's standards. It almost wouldn't be worth working. The longer we waited, the harder the decision got. The thought lingered in my mind all the way to work.

My commute to work took me an hour at the least, depending on traffic. Since I was driving against the Boston commuters, I usually had an easier time, but it was never a guarantee. One bad accident on the Mass Pike or Route 128 and I could easily add another hour to the trip. By the time I got to work, I was ready for something to take my mind off my home problems.

I walked in, expecting a quiet Wednesday night, only to discover that two of my associates hadn't shown up for their shifts. That meant that I would have to close the store with just one other person. I called everyone on my list, but no one could come in to cover. The night ended up being chaotic and it took us nearly double the time to clean the store. I was ready to fall into bed after making the hour-long commute back home, but one look on my husband's face was enough to make me forget my horrible day.

The fact that he was still up was something in itself. He was usually in bed asleep by 9:30 at the latest.

"Where have you been?" he asked me, his eyes narrowed.

I looked down at my work shirt with my nametag still attached. My first inclination was to throw a smart response back at him, but something in his face stopped me.

"I was at work. Why?" I came in and sat on the other end of the couch from him.

He stared straight ahead, his mind obviously on something else.

"What's the matter?" I asked, bracing myself for anything. The last time he was this bad, he asked me for a divorce.

I didn't think that was it, though. Something else seemed to be going on.

Cancer?

A death in the family?

My mind wouldn't stop spinning with suggestions.

He took another swig of his beer, placing it on the coffee table beside the two empties he had already gone through. This wasn't going to be good.

"I lost my job today," he said.

I just sat there and stared at him. While I was relieved he wasn't dying of cancer or asking me for a divorce, it was still staggering news. We could not survive without his paycheck.

My job helped us make our bills, but he made nearly three times the amount I did. Without him working, we were sure to lose everything we had worked so hard for. We didn't have time to talk it over though. We were interrupted by the sound of footsteps on the floor above us, followed by our daughter's piercing scream.

What now? I thought as I raced up the stairs.

16

Laura suffered from acute ear infections. The first one came when she was an infant. Once the colic ceased, the ear issues started.

She would wake up, screaming and holding her ears, but nothing would ease her suffering until we were able to get her to the doctor. He would prescribe an antibiotic and within a few days, the infection would clear and she would be back to normal again before the next one hit.

I inquired about having tubes put in her ears, something they were doing frequently in the early 1990's, but our pediatrician was staunchly against them. He said they could actually cause permanent ear damage down the road and that we were better off just treating each infection. That left us treating ear infections on a constant basis. If it wasn't one ear, it was the other. Sometimes it was both.

I felt so bad for her when she got them. It was obviously excruciating painful. She pulled at her ears and cried, her face turning a deep shade of pink. As we raced upstairs, I was sure it was another ear infection. I began doing a mental inventory of the medicine cabinet in my mind, trying to remember if I had a bottle of children's pain reliever left. What we discovered wasn't even close.

She had backed herself into a corner of the kitchen and was growling at us as we approached.

She looked more like a feral animal than a child.

"Laura?" I said, dropping down to my knees to approach her.

Her face was filled with sheer terror. She looked at me as though I were a snarling monster ready to eat her alive.

"Noooo! Don't!" she screamed, her face wet with tears. Her hair hung down in the mess and she peered at us through the curtain of hair. Her eyes were wild and it was clear that she wasn't seeing us. She was seeing some other reality. Even though she was only four, she was ready to fight to the death.

"Is she dreaming?" my husband asked me.

I reached a hand out towards her and she snarled at me, like a wild animal.

"I think so. Oh my God. What do we do?" I asked, knowing he had less information than I did. She was sleepwalking, just like I did for so many years. She was trapped inside her mind, held tight by a nightmare that would not let her go. There was nothing to do, but wait it out.

We sat on the floor in front of her, soothing her with our words, trying to lure her out of the nightmare. Inside, I was a mess.

What if she didn't come out of it?

Did Gus have a hold on her?

The questions just piled up on top of one another, leaving me in their horrifying wake.

Every time we tried to reach out to touch her, she lashed out with clawed hands. She was down on her hands and knees, as though she were an animal instead of a child. I didn't know what to do.

Was it a seizure? Or some sort of brain malfunction?

I had already read every baby and childcare book I could get my hands on and had never come across anything like it. It was as though my child had turned feral overnight.

After several minutes, she started to come around on her own. It was as though a switch was thrown in her brain. The expression in her eyes changed from panic to confusion as she focused on us for the first time.

"Mommy?" she asked, crawling across the floor to me.

I pulled her into my arms, crying along with her. It had been one of the most terrifying experiences of my life. I cradled her, stroking her soft brown curls and wiping the tears and mucus from her face. She wasn't prone to thumb sucking, but her thumb found her mouth anyway and she fell back asleep in my arms without ever telling us what had happened.

The next morning she was back to normal. I asked her about it several times, but she didn't seem to know what I was talking about. I called our pediatrician as soon as their office was open and made an emergency appointment to have her seen.

Laura hated going to the doctor almost as much as she hated getting ready in the mornings. Considering we had to do both, it was a battle that would leave me on the brink of tears before it was all over. I strapped her into her car seat and just sat for a moment, looking at her in the rear view mirror.

What had happened to my child?

I imagined all sorts of horrible medical conditions. By the time I got to the doctor's office, my brain was on overload. There was nothing worse than having something terrible happen to your child.

They know what scares you.

Was this the work of the ghost in our house? Was he angry that we had started construction again and was lashing out? I looked up to the overcast sky and prayed.

Please do not let this be something awful.

The doctor was a dominant, no-nonsense kind of man. He was curt with his answers and took no more than five minutes to look her over, shining his light in her eyes, and checking her reflexes and vital signs. When he finished, he asked me a few more questions before coming to his conclusion.

"It's night terrors," he said. "Look it up in your baby book or pick up a book at the library. It's just something she will have to outgrow. There's very little you can do about it, but there's nothing wrong with her."

I left his office and went directly to the library, where I checked out several books on sleep disorders. What I found was both reassuring and disheartening at the same time.

Night terrors were a parasomnia disorder, occurring in the first stages of sleep. Patients suffering from it were described as inconsolable and would seemingly wake up with terror in their eyes, their hearts beating rapidly. They would lash out at other people, as if trying to protect themselves from something only they could see. Once they woke up, they would have an amnesiac blackout of the event, not being able to describe what had held them in a terrified grip. It was also congenial, meaning it was passed down from me to my daughter.

It clicked into place for me as I read the last line. I had always thought of my nightmares as bad dreams, not giving them the title of night terrors, but it all made sense. She was suffering from the same nighttime affliction I had years ago. While I still was prone to walking in my sleep, I was much easier to wake up now. Most of the time, I woke myself up by the time I was halfway to the door. I usually just continued on, taking the opportunity to get a drink or use the bathroom, before returning to bed.

Laura's night terrors continued for nearly a year. Each night was a version of the first night. She would race out of bed and find her way into the kitchen, where she would back herself into the corner of the cabinets and fight off anyone who came near her.

As we watched her one night, we were intrigued by the way she looked at us.

"Watch her," my husband said. "She looks at me, and then she looks at something in between us, before she looks at you."

I watched her a little more closely and saw it for myself. It was almost as if someone was standing in between us and she was looking at him before she looked at me. The thought gave me the willies. I moved over to the other side of the kitchen to see if she would follow me with her eyes.

She looked at her father, then at the space beside him, before turning her neck to look at me, leaning against the stove.

"That is so creepy," I said. "It's almost like she's looking at someone who isn't there."

We shared a weighted glance, neither of us willing to say it aloud.

Was it Gus?

Was she looking at a ghost?

We tried to ask her about it when she came out of the night terror, but she never answered us. There was something amnesic about her episodes. When she woke, she was inconsolable for at least ten to fifteen minutes. By the time she finished crying, she couldn't remember anything that had happened to her. The night terrors left her with a black hole in her memory.

"What are we going to do?" I asked him.

He gave me another long look.

"I don't know," he said.

I didn't like the way that sounded. It sounded like we were out of options.

We were at the mercy of an angry ghost.

(Above) Laura and Joni

17

A part of me was relieved that my husband now believed me about Gus.

It was nice to be able to share my concerns with him and not feel as though he was internally measuring me for a strait jacket. After years of hiding in the shadows until he could get me alone, Gus was finally showing himself to my husband as well.

Tools went missing more frequently than before and items around the house began to break. It started with the dishwasher and steadily went from item to item around the house.

We would go into the bathroom to take a shower, only to discover that the hot water heater in the basement was mysteriously been turned off. At first, we blamed it on Laura. She liked to play in the basement. We got her a miniature kitchen for Christmas and she spent hours in it playing house. Since the little kitchen was right outside the door to the laundry room where the hot water heater was located, it wasn't a stretch of the imagination to consider that she might have flipped the switch off until it started happening when Laura wasn't home.

It seemed like it happened at the most inopportune moments, at the time when we needed hot water the most. I'd come home after a strenuous day at work, having dreamt about a hot bath all the way home, only to discover nothing but cold water coming from the tap. Other times, it would happen first thing in the morning, when we had two showers to take.

The construction crew had completed the majority of the work on the house, leaving us with a grand looking Colonial instead of the small blue ranch we'd lived in for almost five years. Things started coming back around for us about the time they finished, packing up their big white truck and leaving us with a shell to finish on our own. My husband found another job, paying him the same amount he made at his last job, and I was offered a brand new store to manage.

My company was planning to open a new store in Waltham, which was just as far away from home as Dedham was for me. While I was elated to have a brand new store to manage, I was sad in realizing I would be spending additional time away from home.

Opening a new store was time-consuming. I'd have to be there from the very beginning, interviewing and hiring a full staff that I would have to also train. I was told we would start in a month. They wanted me to train my current assistant manager to take over for me in Dedham and then start helping in Waltham as they set up the store.

I came home with the news, not sure how my husband was going to take it. A new store was exiting news, but I knew he'd see past the excitement and realize the impact this would have on us. Our relationship was still in a precarious stage. We had good weeks, where we would come together as though nothing bad had ever happened to us, and then we would slide back down that slippery hill to the place where we spun our wheels in the ruts.

Laura ran ahead of me to the door, waiting for me to unlock the door. Before I could, she pointed to the ground.

"Mommy, where's that water coming from?" she asked.

I looked down at the ground to discover water trickling out through the crack under the basement door. I felt my heart lurch at the sight. This couldn't be good.

"Stand back," I told her, moving her over to the side.

I opened the door and a gush of water rushed out, carrying bits of paper and flotsam from the basement along with it. The basement had flooded.

"Oh dear Lord," I whispered under my breath. "Just stay here," I told her and ran to turn the water off."

The hot water heater had burst. Even though it was only a few years old, having been replaced when we bought the house, it had ruptured. The entire basement was flooded with several inches of water.

Something was changing in the house and I wasn't sure where it was going.

18

Something snapped in me after Laura's first night terror episode.

It was bad enough that horrible things were happening to my husband and me. The thought that this entity was now coming after my daughter was more than I could take.

I honestly did not know if her episodes were normal or if they were a result of the ghost in our house. In many ways, it was easier to blame it on the ghost. If it was the ghost, then I could point the finger at the corner of the room instead of pointing it at myself, the mother who passed this abnormality down to her own daughter.

Every night we suffered through them, helpless and lost. I was completely exhausted by the time the episode finally ended. My daughter's expression of outright terror snapped into a look of overwhelming confusion. It as if a light switch was thrown. She went from one emotion to the other in a second.

"Mama?" she said, crawling across the cold linoleum floor, her face covered in tears. She climbed into my arms, sobbing with deep catching breaths that felt like the end of the world.

I held her until the sobs quieted and her little hands let go of their fists, falling limply to her side as she fell back to sleep.

"You bastard!" I screamed at the air the next day before I left for work.

I had been feeling the buzzing sound of him in my ears all morning, almost as though he was mocking me. I held it in until five minutes before I was supposed to leave. I buckled Laura into her car seat, turned on the radio, and went back inside to rant at the ghost.

"You leave her alone. This has nothing to do with her. If you have a problem, you take it out on me or her father, but never on my baby daughter!"

I stood there and stared at the air around me, daring him to show himself. I was ready for a battle. He had crossed a line with me.

After a minute, I turned on my heel and left, slamming the door behind me for good measure.

I don't know if it was a result of my little speech or if it was something that would have normally happened anyway, but the house was quiet for almost a full month afterwards. I didn't sit back and gloat, though. I kept busy. If it was the death of me, I was going to get this ghost out of our house.

I didn't know what to do. I didn't even know where to begin.

If you started telling people you had a ghost in your house, you would be marked as crazy. The books at the library were old and outdated. I even looked in the yellow pages of the phone book to see if there was a paranormal listing, but the closest I found was a listing for psychology, which was where I would have probably ended up if I continued with my quest for knowledge. As it was, the women at the library were giving me disapproving looks when they saw me pulling books from the occult section and bringing them to a reading table.

I was afraid of bringing paranormal books home and tipping Gus off that we were researching him. I don't know why I felt this way, but I was terrified that he would just amp up the activity if he knew I was trying to get rid of him. It was a logical thought. After all, if he was powerful enough to move items and write on a wall, what would prevent him from strangling us in our sleep?

I kept checking the spot beside the fish tank in the basement to see if the words came back, but they remained the same. After the scare with my disk missing and then reappearing, I had all but stopped writing. I even pushed aside my love for scary movies and horror novels and began watching a lighter fare. The last thing I wanted was to give the ghost any advantages.

Most of what he did revolved around fear.

I didn't know why, but he liked to scare us and keep us uneasy. Was it because he enjoyed watching us gasp? Or was it something else? As I spent more and more time at the library, I began to understand a key concept about hauntings. They fed on your fear.

Everything around us was composed of energy. According to Albert Einstein, energy cannot be created or destroyed. It can only be changed from one form to another. If that were true, then what happened to our energy when we died? Did it get absorbed back into the atmosphere or did it remain in the form of a ghost?

Gus's consistent need to scare us made me wonder if it had a deeper meaning. What if he was doing it to fed off our heightened emotions? It seemed like there was a pattern to the activity.

First, there would be a long period of inactivity. Besides the occasional sensation of being watched, nothing else happened. It was as if he was resting up for something. Then, he would do something to scare us. Sometimes it was as simple as a dream, or a dark shadow in a mirror. Soon after that, he would do something to change our behavior.

He didn't like us messing with the basement, but more importantly, he didn't like us being down there at all. That was his space, something he considered sacred. When we started tearing it apart, he saw us as vandals, ripping up all that he'd labored to create. He showed us his displeasure by moving our belongings out of his area. Tools would disappear, power cords would get unplugged, and new wiring would stop working.

It must have been frustrating for him. Despite all his efforts, we continued to push him out. When we began spending more time down in the basement, the activity became explosive.

If that was his intent, then I would happily give him what he wanted.

He could have his damn basement.

The house was large enough for me to avoid the basement. I would just find another space. The basement still gave me the willies, so it wasn't an issue.

The problem was convincing the rest of my family.

The basement was a perfect family room. It was small enough to be cozy, but large enough to accommodate all of us. Instead of crowding on the old couch, we now had an L-shaped sectional sofa that fit us all comfortably. We could sit on it and watch television, while enjoying a nice fire in the fireplace. Many of my daughter's toys were scattered around the room, as well. It was the only place in the house where we could watch television, outside of the small TV we had in our bedroom.

I tried to bring it up to my husband, but he gave me a weary look.

He wasn't letting a ghost chase him out of the family room. He worked far too hard to remodel it to abandon it for the sake of a ghost.

There would have to be another option. Unfortunately, I didn't know what it was.

"I did my best," I whispered to the air. "But, there's nothing else I can do."

I stayed out of the basement as much as possible, but it wasn't enough for our grumpy ghost. I began to get the feeling that the basement wasn't enough for him. He wanted us out of the house altogether.

Before he sent us out, he had something else up his sleeve.

Since he now knew what scared me, he would bring it to a whole new level.

He would take something from me that would bring me to my knees.

It was only a matter of time.

(Above) the finished basement

19

I didn't know I was pregnant until I was in the process of losing the baby.

The owners of the pet supply chain sent me to help with a neighboring store that was relocating to a new building. I wasn't eager to be there. The work was hot and gritty, involving hand loading boxes of product into trucks. I carried one heavy box after another, feeling the pull of muscles in my lower back.

By mid-day, I began feeling an odd sensation in my lower abdomen. It wasn't anything I'd ever experienced before, so I took a break. I sat for a moment and sipped on my coffee, then headed to the bathroom before I planned to return to work. What I found left me shaken. I was bleeding heavily.

I left work and made an appointment with my doctor for the following day. In the meantime, I stopped by the pharmacy on my way home and picked up a pregnancy test.

My fingers fumbled as I tried to open the box as a mixture of emotions hit me square on. I wasn't sure I was ready for a baby right now. I was getting ready to open a brand new store, one that would require all my energy.

If my condition was typical of my pregnancy with Laura, I would be so exhausted I'd struggle just to make it through each day. I would also be physically limited. I couldn't pick up a bag of dog food unless it was under ten pounds. I couldn't move fixtures from one area to another. I would be virtually useless at a time when my employers were expecting my best.

I was also uneasy about my present condition. I wasn't nauseated. My breasts weren't tender. I hadn't gained so much as a pound. Most of all, my energy level was normal. If I were truly pregnant, wouldn't I be feeling some of these symptoms?

The sense of elation was missing as I took the test. It made me think of the last time I took a pregnancy test when I was pregnant with Laura. I had been so overjoyed, praying with my whole heart that the test would be positive. Now, I wasn't certain what I hoped for.

A positive reading came with complications. Life would become difficult, given my current circumstances, but a negative reading wouldn't leave me any happier.

All my life, I imagined having two children. When I closed my eyes and thought about them, I saw myself with two girls. They would be close enough in age to enjoy one another's company, but would be far enough apart to enjoy having ample attention as babies.

I watched mothers struggle with toddlers who were close in age and never considered that a route I wanted to pursue. As soon as one weaned from the breast, another came along to claim it. It seemed exhausting for the mother and unfair for the older child, who would have to relinquish her mother's undivided attention at such a young age.

If I had a perfect time frame, I probably would have chosen three to four years. As it was, we were already a year past that. A baby born now would be five years younger than Laura. The longer we waited, the larger this gap grew.

I carried the test to the kitchen and sat down at the table where I could look out at the backyard. The glorious apple trees were in full bloom, sending cascades of pink flower petals to the ground with every brush of the wind. Fat bees lumbered over the blossoms, filling the air with the sound of their buzzing.

My ears began ringing at that moment. I looked around me, expecting to see him, as I always did. His presence was so decisive to me. I could feel him there so strongly, watching me.

Sometimes I could feel his moods. It seemed strange to me that a ghost would have moods, but I couldn't deny the feelings that washed through me whenever he was near. Most of the time, he was just disgusted and grumpy. Other times, he was outright furious. This time, his emotion was almost toxic. He was smug.

It was as if he knew something I didn't and was taunting me with the knowledge.

I sighed. "Just leave me alone, Gus. I have bigger things to worry about now," I said, thinking about all the changes we would have to make. How would we survive on just one income while I was on maternity leave? I barely had two weeks of vacation left. That left three or four weeks without a paycheck. Was I really ready for this?

The timer on the microwave beeped, signifying the end of the test.

I pushed away from the chair and turned off the timer, still carrying the test stick in my hand. I cradled it against my chest, closing my eyes against everything it would tell me, of all the life-altering changes I would soon face.

I opened my eyes and took a deep breath and then looked at the stick.

It was positive.

I just stared at it for a moment, letting the results sink in.

I was pregnant.

I put my hand on my stomach, as if to comfort the child against my earlier misgivings. I was sorry for feeling inconvenienced, for thinking for even a second that I didn't want this child. Suddenly, nothing was more important in my life than bringing this child into the world. If I allowed my work schedule to dictate the timing for another child, there would never be a good time. There would always be something to hold me back. This was good.

This was better than good. It was wonderful.

I allowed a smile to unfurl on my face, feeling it radiate through me, filling me with happiness. I started towards the phone, wanting to share my unexpected news with my husband, when I was bowled over with pain. Something was wrong.

I looked down to see my khaki pants saturated with blood.

In that moment, I knew what was happening. I was losing the baby before I even had a chance to absorb the reality.

I called my doctor and she wanted to see me immediately. I changed my pants and rushed to the office, not feeling like I could even take the time to call my husband first. It was always a lengthy process. I had to call the car dealership where he worked and ask the operator for his number. Then she would transfer me to his department, where they would page him. The precious minutes it would take would only delay me. I needed to get to the office quickly.

As I made my way down the basement stairs, I could feel Gus tagging along behind me.

This is what you get for messing with me.

I stopped with my hand on the door, praying he was wrong.

Unfortunately he wasn't.

I went through the following days in mourning. By my own estimation, the baby would have been born right around my birthday in March.

I felt the loss deeply. I carried it with me through every waking moment of the day. I found myself breaking down into tears at the sight of mothers with babies. I threw away all the magazines on my coffee table, not wanting to see anything that might remind me of my loss. People tried to comfort me, but it only made it worse.

You can always try again, they said, causing a sense of anger to wash over me. It was as if they were saying that this life wasn't special, that it could be replaced by another. How could that be possible?

It wasn't as if I would have another chance with this one. This baby was gone before it could even be a reality.

I never knew if it was a boy or a girl, but somehow inside I held the answer. I saw a blond little girl in my dreams. She smiled shyly at me as she looked up with bright blue eyes. Laura would have loved her. The two would have played dress-up together in the pink room they shared. She would have been quieter than my Laura, more of an observer than a leader, someone Laura would have taken to quickly. I saw her shy smile in my mind and I loved her without every knowing her.

I returned to work after only a few days. Sitting around the house only served to remind me of my misery. I would rather stay busy, keeping my mind occupied with something other than the thought of the loss.

I never considered that Gus might have had anything to do with it. It seemed too enormous for him to touch, even though it was obvious he knew about the outcome before I did. I just tucked it into the back of my mind, along with all the other tragedies we suffered in that house. It wouldn't feel relevant until years later when I piled them all up and considered them as a whole.

Life was full of loss, but it felt like we had more than our share during our years in that house. If this made Gus happy, I'd never know. All I knew was that he wanted us to leave and would do anything he could to make it happen.

20

As summer deepened, it brought with it the heat and humidity of August. The days became endlessly long as I helped at the store that was relocating. The air conditioning wasn't functional until several days prior to their grand opening, so we spent the time sweltering inside the concrete box, wiping sweat from our eyes as we moved product from the boxes to their proper locations on the shelves.

Under normal situations, I would have enjoyed the creative pleasure of merchandising. I had a knack for arranging the items in an eye-pleasing fashion, but the pleasure would be lost on me as I recovered from my loss. All I could think about was how everything changed in the blink of an eye.

It could have gone either way. Had it worked out for the positive, I would have been smiling to myself, keeping a secret that I wouldn't share with anyone for weeks. I would have touched my stomach, holding my hand over the tiny life budding inside me. The reality was simply the absence of all of those things and the guilt that clung to it, like a fine outer layer.

Had I done something wrong? Did I lift something that was too heavy? I should have eaten better and slept more. I could have done many things differently had I known about the life inside of me. I berated myself for not paying more attention to my cycle. I should have caught it at five weeks instead of eight. I also labored over the way I teetered as I waited for the test results, a part of me hoping for a negative result. Had I jinxed this poor baby before it ever got a chance?

I just kept to myself, not knowing anyone well enough to attempt socialization. I kept my loss to myself,

Devil's Toy Box

not sharing it with anyone other than the woman in Human Resources who took my initial call when I needed to request several days off. I pulled pet supplies out of boxes and put them on shelves, barely paying attention to what I was doing. By the end of August, they were finally ready to move me to my new store and I could not have been happier.

It was a good change of pace for me. I would be too busy to think about my personal life. There was so much work to do. Going through the relocation with the other store gave me an advantage with the new store, since I now knew what needed to be completed. It was just a matter of doing it.

Having a new store put me in a prestigious position, at least in my own mind. I reassured myself that the owners wouldn't give new stores to managers they didn't think could handle it. They alluded to the possibility of having even bigger plans for me in the future. They wanted to use me as a recovery manager, sending me to stores with issues and having me fix them. I would train a manager and then be sent to another location. Eventually, this might lead me to a district manager position. I couldn't have been happier. I liked having a goal to reach for, and I needed the boost of confidence that came with it.

When I arrived at the Waltham store for the first time, I sat in the parking lot staring at the sight in front of me, wondering what my life was going to be like now. Up until that point, I ran smaller stores that had an established customer base and experienced employees. Here, I would be starting from scratch on every level.

The building was an old abandoned grocery store, with a long bank of dirty windows along the front. It was anchored on one side by several other smaller buildings.

One would be a coffee shop, while the other would become a drug store. By all rights, it should have been a wildly successful location, but I didn't like it.

Something about it seemed off.

I finally got out of my car and walked inside. The temperature dropped by at least ten degrees as I crossed over the threshold. I could feel a faint breeze wafting through the space, bringing with it the stench of rot and decay. It was apparent that the building was abandoned for a number of years. It had a feeling of neglect, as though it was locked away and forgotten.

The ceilings were long gone, leaving the overhead metal beams as canopies for the decades of cobwebs that draped over them. The floors were covered with fifty-year-old tiles. Most of them were faded and cracked, if not missing altogether. As I stood there taking it all in, I had to wonder if the place was also haunted.

What would keep someone trapped in our world?

I knew from the books I'd read that when people die they are supposed to cross over into a white light and moved into another dimension commonly known as Heaven, but some souls hesitate. They look at the white light, but then turned back to take stock in the life they were leaving behind. Instead of finding the salvation and serenity they deserved, they chose to remain in the land of the living.

How horrible would that be? They imprison themselves in a world filled with living people without a body to navigate with. They would be able to watch us move through our lives, but they would have to remain in the shadows as observers. Was that what happened to Gus? Did he choose to remain behind to guard his beloved house?

I walked deeper into the interior, allowing my eyes to adjust to the lack of lighting. The morning sun only reached so far through the front windows, leaving the rest of the building lost in shadows.

"Hello?" I called out. People were supposed to be meeting me here, but it might take me a while to find them in the massive building.

"We're down here," someone called from a hallway on the right.

I followed the hallway to a doorway that led down to a basement. Even though the stairs were dusty and worn, the space below them was lit brightly from the ancient overhead fixtures. I made my way down to them, finding them in a large room at the bottom of the stairs.

"What do you think? Wouldn't this make a great break room?" one of them asked.

I looked around and arched my eyebrows. I couldn't imagine wanting to spend time in here relaxing, but it had potential.

Once we cleared away the dirt and debris, it might look more inviting. It made me think about seeing my house for the first time and how the realtor told us that a fresh coat of paint and our own furniture would change it dramatically. In some ways she was right, but she was wrong in other ways. A coat of paint could not fix haunted.

My initial team consisted of three people. I would have two assistant managers and a warehouse manager. My two assistants were hired for me, something that initially made me a little worried. Since I would be working very closely with them, I needed to make sure we would all be able to work cohesively as a team, but the owners had already promoted them from other stores.

As it turned out, I shouldn't have worried. My two assistant managers were exactly who I needed. One was a twenty-five year old woman named Pam, who came from a nearby sister store. She had been with the company for years and had a good eye for product merchandising. My other assistant manager was a woman named Sabrina, who preferred to be called Bree. She was in her early twenties and was a small sprite of a woman with curly brown hair.

The third member of my team was Will, who would be my warehouse manager. His job was to oversee all of our incoming shipments and insuring the product was put away in a timely manner. Will had been with the company for years, starting as a stock person, then moving into store set-ups as they opened more locations. I was happy to have him working with me.

I would build from there, setting up interviews for later in the week. To start though, we were going to be sitting in the basement putting price labels on product. It seemed like a foolhardy gesture to me. Wouldn't it be easier to price the items as we put them on the shelves? This meant we would have to handle the product twice. It didn't make any sense to me, but I wasn't left with any other options. I had to do what the owners wanted us to do.

We went down the stairs to the basement and began exploring the rooms. It was a literal maze down there. One room led to another in a succession that didn't make any sense. There were two full locker rooms, complete with showers and bathroom stalls. Just off those rooms were two other rooms that might have once been break rooms for the grocery store employees. The part that intrigued me the most were the tunnels.

To get to them, you had to pass through a pitch-black area of the basement. Old wooden shelving with chicken wire backing lined the room. My tiny flashlight barely made a dent into the darkness as we walked through, fielding off spider webs and cold chills.

"I heard that they found a dead person down here," Bree said with a shaky voice. Her words stopped me in mid-step. "Really? When?"

"I don't know. I think it was years ago. Homeless people used to come down here after the grocery store went out of business. See all the liquor bottles?" she said, pointing to the corner where a pile of nip bottles glimmered in the light.

Her words gave me the chills. If someone died down here, there was a possibility that his ghost remained. The last thing I needed was another ghost on my hands. I kept my thoughts to myself and continued on through the tunnel until it came to a locked door at the end.

"That leads to the drug store," Bree said. She pointed to another door just to the left. "That door leads to the coffee shop. They have them locked. We already tried to get in," she said with a grin.

We spent the remainder of the week in the basement, pricing product and then throwing it into boxes. I never felt any ghostly presences, but I was too preoccupied to notice. It was tedious work and we grew cold from sitting on the damp concrete floor. By the end of the week, I was feeling out of sorts. My back began to ache and my energy was diminished down to almost nothing. I was sicker than I had been when I was pregnant.

What was wrong with me?

I was forced to call in sick on the fifth morning. I barely had the energy to drag myself out of bed and the pain in my back had worsened. It felt as though a knife was wedged in between my shoulder blades. I called the doctor and went in for an exam, only to find out I had pneumonia.

It would take me out of work for a full week.

I was back home with Gus.

And as it turns out, he was waiting for me.

21

The week I spent on the couch would have been a fog for me if Gus hadn't been there to keep me busy. I was on a heavy round of painkillers for the first few days, which kept me moderately sedated and incoherent. During this time, I remember very little except for the dreams.

The mirrors in the house had been bothering me for a long time. Even though I loved the way they moved light around the room, making a smaller room look larger and brighter, they also reflected more than the images in front of them. I often caught glimpses of something in the mirrors that I couldn't explain. It was if something darted out of sight as I looked up.

I began avoiding them. If I needed to check my appearance, I went into the bathroom and looked in the mirror above the sink. It was the only mirror in the house that felt safe. The others seemed like windows to the spirit world, a concept that would solidify for me in the next few days.

I began having strange dreams about mirrors. At first, I blamed it on the painkillers. My dreams were abnormally vivid, almost as real as true life. Instead of having my normal nightmares, where an unseen man was chasing me in the darkness, I began having dreams about ghostly beings stepping in and out of the mirrors.

From my research at the library, I knew that mirrors had long been associated with the paranormal. Some mediums used them for something called scrying. They would sit in a dimly lit room with a mirror in front of them and stare at the image, willing it to show them their future. Others said that ghosts used them as portals to the other side, stepping in and out of them at will. I hadn't given it much thought until I began seeing things in my own mirrors.

I collected gold framed mirrors. I had at least a dozen of them around the house in various rooms. Even though I rarely looked into them, not wanting to see the haggard reflection of my tired self, I often caught glimpses of movement just behind me. Were the books correct? Could mirrors be doorways for the afterlife, giving them easy access to my house? The dreams I started having during my week on the couch made me consider it.

The first dream came at the tail end of my usual nightmare. Someone was chasing me through a dark tunnel. As I ran, casting glances over my shoulder to see how close he was, I nearly stumbled on something on the ground. When I turned, I found myself in front of a massive mirror.

My terrified face stared back at me. As I watched in horror, the black shadow rushed up behind me from the darkness, his features merging with my own, altering my face into something terrifying. When I woke up, I was sitting on the bathroom sink, staring at myself in the mirror.

I jumped with a start and swiveled around to look behind me.

All I saw was the floral shower curtain. I pulled it back, almost expecting to find something standing there, but the tub was empty. It took me hours to get back to sleep.

What had it meant?

Was the evil man from our house trying to scare me, or did it go even deeper? Was he trying to take me over as well? The thought terrified me.

Devil's Toy Box

What would happen if I started doing more than walking in my sleep? It was obvious that he was manipulating me and my daughter in our sleep. Could he do more than make us just run through the house? My daughter came into the bathroom all sleepy-eyed and sweet. She was usually the first one up in the morning and seemed surprised to see me.

"Mommy, can you play with me?" she asked. Even though I still felt like I had broken glass inside my lungs, I couldn't resist.

"Of course. Can you bring some Barbies to the couch and we can play in there?" I asked.

She smiled and scampered off into her bedroom to retrieve the dolls, complete with clothing and shoes. Accessorizing her dolls was always her top priority. For Christmas, she told several relatives that she was hoping to get Barbie shoes from Santa, which resulted in nearly a hundred shoes. By May, nearly half of them were already lost.

She snuggled up on the couch with me and we played with her dolls until it was time for breakfast. I was so thankful she was getting older and could entertain herself for longer periods, especially when I felt so horrible. I fixed her a bowl of cereal and turned on the small TV in the kitchen, tuned in to her favorite cartoon and she was quiet for almost a half hour.

I sunk back down into the couch and closed my eyes, listening to the sound of the television in the other room. I looked around the room, wondering if anything could help me. I wasn't a religious person. I spent a childhood fidgeting my way through Sunday church services, but I hadn't been to church in years. My husband was Catholic and I was Protestant. We tried going to each other's churches, but just never found one that felt right for both of us, so we gave up. It didn't mean that I didn't believe in God. I just came to realize that I didn't need to be inside a church to worship.

Before I went to bed each night, I had a ritual I went through. I said the Lord's Prayer in my mind, followed by a quick personal prayer. I thought about all the people in my life that meant so much to me and I asked God to bless them. It hadn't occurred to me to ask for protection.

I closed my eyes and said a brief prayer, hoping it would help.

Please help me find a way to protect us from this entity.

Before I knew it, I had fallen back asleep. I feel right back into a dream.

In my dream, I was again running through a dark tunnel, trying to get away from someone. As I neared the end of the tunnel, in the place where he always caught up to me, I saw a light radiating down another branch of the tunnel that I didn't notice before. Something about it drew me closer.

I stopped running, feeling the dregs of fear falling off me. As I got closer to the light, I could see that it was coming from a woman. She was holding a candle at the end of the tunnel. As I got closer, I started making out her features. It was my grandmother, Nanny.

She smiled at me, holding my gaze for a long moment, before she looked down and touched something silver that hung from a chain around her neck. I only got a quick glimpse of it before the image faded and I found myself waking. It was a pocket watch.

I awoke to find Laura standing in front of me, marching her Barbies across my arm.

"Mommy, I'm bored. Can we go play in my room?" she asked.

I loved her with all my heart, but the last thing I wanted to do was to go play Barbies in her room with her, considering how sick I felt. Try as I may though, I couldn't say no. Maybe a compromise would suffice.

"If I come in and play with you for a few minutes, do you think you could let Mommy lay down for a little bit while you watch a movie? Mommy doesn't feel well," I told her.

She nodded, happy to have a playmate.

My husband and I had talked about having another child for a long time. After the miscarriage, the subject was swiftly dropped, but it still lingered in my mind. While our marriage wasn't the strongest, we knew that we needed to hold onto it, if nothing else but for the sake of our daughter.

The separation had been rough on her and I hated putting her through anything else. We also didn't want her growing up as an only child. It always made me think about my own mother, who hadn't had any siblings. When her parents died within years of each other, she was completely alone in the world, except for her two daughters. I didn't want Laura to ever feel that way. She was often lonely and I hated that.

We played for nearly an hour, until I reached a place where I just couldn't handle any more. I set her up with a video and left her to watch it, while I went to lay back down. As I walked to my room, I remembered the dream about my grandmother.

Nanny and I always had a special bond. Before we moved to the A-frame, we lived in a little log cabin across a pond from my grandparents. I would walk across the dam to their house daily, just to spend time with them.

Nanny spoiled me rotten, buying me anything and everything I wanted. She would cook special meals for me and would read to me as we sat in her rocking chair by the door. When she died when I was just six years old, it was traumatic for all of us.

The day after she died, I had a curious dream about her.

In the dream, my mother and I were going to clean out her room. My mother wanted to bring some of her clothes to the Goodwill so my grandfather wouldn't have to deal with it. As we came into her house, I was shocked to find her sitting on her living room couch, smiling at me.

My mother walked right past her, not seeing her sitting there, which shocked me. I tried to call after her, but she had already disappeared into Nanny's bedroom.

I approached Nanny on the couch. I was so happy to see her, but I was confused at the same time.

"I thought you died, Nanny," I told her.

She smiled down at me. "I did, but I couldn't leave without saying goodbye to you," she told me, and then I awoke from the dream.

I carried that dream around with me for years, thinking about it and wondering if it had been more than merely a dream. I often felt like she was still around, watching over me. Once, I really think she saved me from a near fatal accident.

When it happened, I was seventeen years-old. I was driving home from a job interview and was speeding a little faster than necessary, hoping to get back in time to see my boyfriend before he left for work. Suddenly, the image of Nanny popped into my head, telling me to slow down.

The thought was so abrupt, I couldn't help but listen. I pulled my foot off the gas and pressed the brakes. Seconds later, my front tire blew out. As I coasted to the breakdown lane, I thanked my lucky stars and my grandmother for saving me. Had I been going seventy miles an hour when the tire blew out, my car probably would have careened out of control.

The latest dream about her had been startling. I hadn't dreamt of her in years. The strangest part about it was the necklace she showed me in the dream. I had one just like it in my bedroom. It had been in my jewelry box for as long as I could remember, but I didn't know where it had come from. My mother might have given it to me years ago, but I wasn't sure. Even though I wanted nothing more than to collapse on my bed and fall into a dreamless slumber, I went to my jewelry box and found the pocket watch.

It was old and worn, the silver backing showing years of use. I tried to wind it, but the time was stuck at 8:21. Something about it gave me comfort, though. I slipped it around my neck before I found my way to bed. I slept for nearly two full hours before Laura appeared beside my bed, wanting lunch.

Maybe Nanny was still with me.

It gave me hope, something I desperately needed.

22

    The doctor gave me a clean bill of health a week later, along with the approval to return to work. I could have easily used another week off to regain my energy, but I felt as though I had missed enough work to put me behind schedule. I didn't want to miss any more.

    I needed to go through the piles of applications and start scheduling interviews, so I could hire more staff. My goal was to have them train at another store prior to our grand opening and I wanted to give them ample time.

    As soon as I walked in the door, my set-up crew crowded around me, wanting to show me all the progress they had made in my absence. The building was starting to look like a pet store. The changes were amazing. While I was disappointed I wasn't there for the process, I was pleased with the results and proud of my team.

    The workers had patched the walls and floor, adding in droplights that hung from the ceiling, lighting every square inch of the building. Most of the shelving units were constructed and were being placed according to a master floor plan. The boxes of product we had price in the basement, leading to my bout of pneumonia, were sitting in each aisle, ready to be placed on the shelves. The bank of aquariums had also arrived and the plumbers were busy hooking it up. I was pleased that everything was falling into place.

    I began putting in seventy-hour weeks, trying to keep us on schedule. I felt guilty for missing so much work in the very beginning, first with the miscarriage and then with pneumonia. Even though I couldn't have prevented either situation, it still put me in a bad position. Retail management was an unforgiving profession. The store had to open on schedule, despite any problems I might be having. The only way to make it up would be to put in extra hours.

I came home long after everyone had gone to bed and often left the house before anyone else woke up. My husband wasn't happy with the situation, but I didn't have any other choices. If I was going to remain in retail management, I would have to start making more sacrifices, especially in running a new store. I wasn't any happier about it than he was. I missed tucking my daughter into bed and talking with my family over dinner.

We were lucky that my husband's two sisters, Audra and Cindy had moved to our town and were able to take turns picking Laura up from daycare. Audra often stayed with Laura at our house, fixing her dinner and playing with her until my husband came home from work.

I missed my daughter like crazy, but didn't have any other choices. I was needed at the store during that critical time, which meant I couldn't be at home.

It didn't seem to bother Laura though. She loved spending time with her Aunt Audra, who endlessly doted on her. By this time, the night terrors had all but disappeared at that point, as had the ear infections that had plagued her since birth. She slept through the nights, giving me a solid night of rest once I found my way home. If I dreamed, I don't remember. I slipped through the door after everyone else had gone to bed and I collapsed until my alarm woke me the following morning.

My fatigue gave me a distance from the haunting at my house. If he tried to get to me, I didn't notice. I crawled home on the wings of exhaustion and then crawled back out again only slightly better. I didn't fully wake up until midday when the caffeine kicked in, and even then I was too preoccupied to notice anything out of the ordinary. My employees noticed, though. Bree found me in the back room, sorting through a box.

"Hey, you know we have a ghost in the basement, right?" she asked.

I looked up so quickly, I nearly made myself dizzy.

"A ghost?"

She smiled, making the dimples on her cheeks appear. She reminded me a little of a porcelain doll with her creamy skin, bright blue eyes and curly brown hair.

"Yes, a ghost," she said, and then went on to tell me that many of the employees we'd recently hired wouldn't go down into the basement.

"Has anybody seen anything?" I asked, curious by the information. I too had felt a little creeped out down there, but it was a very creepy place. The feelings seemed appropriate for the situation.

"No, not really. They just don't like the way it feels," she said.

Under normal circumstances, I wouldn't have shared my personal information with her, but given my exhaustion, I found myself telling her about the ghost in my house. When I finished, she looked at me with wide eyes.

"My boyfriend reads a lot of books about that ghost stuff. Let me talk to him and see what he thinks you should do," she said.

I agreed and thought very little about it again over the course of the next few days.

When I had to go down to the basement, I began giving it a better examination. It was the kind of spot you expected to find a ghost, but I didn't feel anything other than the chill of ill ease. My ears didn't ring and I found myself thinking more about human predators who might be hiding behind the old shelves than paranormal intruders.

When Bree's boyfriend stopped in at the end of my shift one day, I took a few minutes and talked with him. We went down to the break room to sit and chat. I purchased a soft drink from the machine we had installed and offered him one as well, but he declined it.

"I have to get to work myself soon. I just wanted to hear more about your ghost and see if I could offer any suggestions," he said.

He was so different from Bree, it was hard to see them as a couple. While she was short and round, he was tall and thin, with close-cut dark hair and dark-framed glasses. He reminded me of the nerdy kid in high school who ran the debate team.

I told him about Gus, giving him the overview of the activity. When I was finished, he narrowed his eyes.

"Have you told him that he needs to leave? Have you claimed your space?" he asked.

The thought alone was enough to make me nearly rise out of my chair. "No, of course not. I don't want to make him any angrier than he already is. Wouldn't that be a bad thing to do?" I asked.

He pursed his lips to the side, giving me an incredulous look. "Only if you want to keep him there. I'm assuming you don't," he said and waited for me to shake my head. "Then stand your ground with him or he's just going to get worse."

I wasn't sure what to make of his advice. I knew from my own research that doing the wrong thing was worse than doing nothing at all. Things had quieted down for the moment at home and the last thing I wanted to do was to stir things up again.

I decided to wait and see what happened.

Now that I had figured out the pattern, it felt as though I might be able to do something about it. If he was using fear to illicit a response from us, which in turn gave him more energy to be more active, then we would just stop feeding him.

I would try very hard to stop gasping at every dark shadow. I would simply turn my head and pretend I didn't see it. If I didn't give him what he needed, then I might possibly stop the chain of events.

It seemed like a good plan at the time.

Time would only serve to prove me wrong.

23

I didn't tell Laura's Aunt Audra about the haunting. The last thing I wanted was for her to feel fearful when she was in the house. Initially, Gus had only shown himself to me, adding my husband into his private club years later. I thought that it would take him a while before he became comfortable enough with Audra to show himself to her as well, but I was wrong.

I received a frantic phone call from her one afternoon.

I was in my office, going over an order I needed to place when the cashier paged me on the store intercom, telling me I had a phone call. I picked up the phone and could barely make out what she was saying.

"I think someone broke into your house," she told me. "All the doors were open and the lights were on."

I closed my eyes and buried my face in my hands. What should I tell her?

I wasn't sure she would be relieved to learn it was a ghost instead of a burglar, but I also didn't want to gloss over the situation in case it wasn't what I thought it was. If it truly was a burglar, and I sent her in the house, passing it off as one of Gus's pranks, it could lead to a dangerous situation for them.

"Where are you now?" I asked.

"I took Laura to my place. I didn't want to take the chance and go inside in case someone was there," she said. "Should I call the police?"

I took a deep breath. "No. Your brother should be home in a few minutes. Let's let him go through the house first and see if he thinks it was a break in or not," I told her.

"What else would it be?" she asked. "You wouldn't have left the house with all three doors wide open, would you?"

I wasn't sure how she was going to react to the news, but it was time to fill her in on what was going on.

"I think we have a ghost. This has happened before," I told her.

She took the news well. If anything, she seemed reluctant to believe the ghost story. I wasn't sure if that was good or bad. Gus had let my husband go for over a year before showing him any signs of his presence, but then again, I'm pretty sure he was doing that to alienate me. If Audra was too vocal about not believing in him, I was afraid he might start trying to prove his point.

My husband came home an hour later and checked the house, only to find it empty, as I knew it would be. I didn't know what he told his sister. More than likely, he laughed it off or told her that I must have been absentminded as I left the house that morning. Either way, it didn't matter because Gus would repeat his mischief again and again, forcing the issue.

The one thing that mattered to me was keeping this knowledge away from Laura. Since the night terrors had disappeared, she hadn't shown any signs of knowing Gus was in the house. The last thing I wanted to do was scare her. I knew what it was like to live in a haunted house. I didn't want to share that experience with her if I could help it.

It made me wonder about the heredity of an ability like mine. I knew there was something different about me. Since I was a child, I had been sensing ghosts. This wasn't something that happened to most people.

I had to wonder if it was something that was passed down from mother to child, like green eyes and freckles. I hoped that wasn't the case. My parents didn't seem to have any ability, so it seemed strange to me that I ended up this way.

The one thing that came to mind was all the testing they did when I first started getting migraines. They hooked me up to electrodes and they put me in cat scanning machines. Could the electricity or magnetism used in these devices have prompted my abilities or was it something I was just naturally born with? I didn't have any clear answers, except for the fact that I saw the ghost in my father's house before all that began. It didn't make any sense to me.

If my husband and sister-in-law hadn't experienced some of Gus's hijinks, I might have wondered if I was just crazy. While I wasn't happy that he was actively scaring everyone, it was reassuring to know that I wasn't the only one experiencing his haunting.

I came home later that evening to find everyone already asleep in bed. I was exhausted from a full day of working, but I needed some time to myself.

Bree's boyfriend's words haunted my mind, but I didn't have the energy to do anything with them. I closed my eyes and rested my head against the back of the couch, wondering what we were going to do.

"Gus, just please leave us alone," I whispered, hoping against hope that he would abide by my words.

24

Six months later, I was transferred from the Waltham store to another location. Ironically, it was full circle for me. They sent me back to the store where I started my employment as a cashier.

I was initially dismayed, not getting the opportunity to enjoy all the work I'd put into the new store, but there were perks to being back in Natick. I was much closer to home. Instead of driving over an hour to work each day, my commute was now a half-hour.

The staff at the Natick store was experienced, allowing me more time away. I no longer needed to work sixty-hour weeks. I could put in my normal forty hours and spend the rest of the time with my family, which was just as well. Soon after I relocated, I discovered I was pregnant.

All the old fears returned as I thought about the miscarriage I suffered. Would this baby be stolen from me, as well?

Thankfully, the activity at home had slowed down. I wasn't certain if my words to Gus made an impact or if he was merely saving his energies for a future bombardment. Either way, it gave me the time I needed to rest and enjoy my family.

I went on maternity leave two weeks before my due date, hoping to ready the house for a new baby. Three other women in my neighborhood had also been pregnant over the summer. One by one, they gave birth, showing off their newborns with a happiness I yearned for.

It was the hottest summer in recent years, something that was impacted by the lack of air conditioning in our house. We had one window unit in our bedroom, but the rest of the house was boiling hot. The only other place I had to retreat to was the cool basement, but I didn't want to go down there.

By mid-August, I was so miserable I was ready for the agony of childbirth. I didn't care how much it hurt. I simply wanted to be finished with pregnancy.

I was tired of being so large. My ankles were so swollen, there was little division between my legs and my feet. I was one big swollen blob of humanity.

Trevor finally made his appearance into the world during the last week of August. I couldn't have been happier.

He was so perfect, I couldn't stop looking at him. He was fair-haired like me, but had his father's dark brown eyes. When I took him shopping, people constantly stopped me, telling me what a beautiful baby he was. They called him a little Buddha baby due to his perfectly round head. His hair was slow to grow in, leaving him nearly bald until he was two years old.

Laura loved her baby brother and was helpful with his care. When it came time to go back to work, I balked. How could I leave my children in the hands of daycare workers? I figured it out on paper and realized that I would be bringing home very little income after paying for two children's daycare fees.

I talked it over with my husband and we agreed that I would stay home with the children for a while. I could work part-time evening shifts at a local restaurant to help with the bills.

Laura started kindergarten that fall, while I stayed home with my new baby. I cherished the time with him, not having had the opportunity with Laura.

He was an easy baby, but like his sister, he refused to nap. While my neighbors with babies chatted and enjoyed hours of gardening while their babies slept, I played with Trevor on the lawn, trying to garden one handed, like I did previously with his sister.

Gus seemed to retreat into the background.

Occasionally, I would find an item missing, but with two children in the house, along with their friends, it was difficult to determine if it was paranormal or just normal behavior.

We finished the majority of the renovations on the house, carving out brand new bedrooms on the second floor and turning the downstairs bedrooms into an office and a playroom for the kids.

The carpeting was removed and the hardwood floors were sanded and polished, making the house look brand new. My husband build a staircase of solid oak that led to the second floor. The only thing we didn't finish was the two upstairs bathrooms. We decided to hold off on the project until we had more money.

I was still working nights, waitressing. I despised the job, but it enabled me to spend the day with my children, so I put up with it.

In the meantime, I got busy writing again. I finished my first book in 1999, a dreadful mystery called Gerald's Dead. I didn't even try to get it published. I passed it along to several of my friends and neighbors and then moved onto the next book I wanted to write.

Life was finally good for us. Our family was strong. We went on camping trips together and spent our weekends working on home improvement projects. Our children were bright and happy and everything seemed to finally be falling into place for us.

Everything changed in an instant when Trevor was two years old. That was when my husband brought up the subject of moving.

If Gus didn't like us there, he didn't want us to leave either. Life turned into a nightmare on the turn of a dime.

(Above) Joni with Trevor and her mother, Charlotte

25

I dug my heels in when my husband first proposed the idea of moving. I was happy where we were. After ten years in Westborough, I finally had made a few close friends. The kids were happy and our lives had settled into a contentment I treasured.

His argument was that Westborough was growing far too rapidly, something I couldn't argue with. Large developments were moving in at a rapid pace, replacing all the open land with subdivisions and more people.

The schools were overloaded. By the time my daughter made it to fifth grade, the grade school was too overpopulated. They moved her class to the old middle school and moved the middle school to the top floor of the high school.

Even driving to the grocery store became a nightmare. The two miles that separated us from town began taking upwards of twenty minutes to navigate, due to all the excess traffic.

"We could sell the house and make a fortune," he told me. "Then, we could build our dream house in the country."

We spent weekends driving from town to town, trying to find one that met all our needs. We wanted something out in the country, but still within range of my husband's work. He'd been transferred to a dealership in Worcester, which allowed us to consider towns further west.

A realtor showed us plots of land in various towns, but a newspaper article led us to Oakham. A new neighborhood was under construction and the perfect lot was available.

Oakham was located twenty-seven miles north-west of Westborough in a heavily wooded area. The town itself was small and quaint, without a single grocery store or gas station within the town limits. In many ways, it reminded me of my hometown of Wadesville, Indiana. I fell in love with it in an instant.

We put a deposit down on the land and began to design our dream home, not aware that our conversations were monitored by a ghostly presence.

Within days, Gus's activity became unbearable.

Items didn't simply get misplaced, they disappeared altogether. We began hearing footsteps on the first floor while we sat in the basement. Several times the toilet flushed on its own accord.

It was getting harder and harder to hide the haunting from Laura. By this time, she was seven years old and was more aware of her environment. When the paranormal activity grew stronger, she looked at me with wide eyes, asking me what was going on.

I held her off until she saw Gus for herself. After that, there was no pretending we didn't have a ghost in our house

Laura and I sat in the basement watching a movie while Trevor played with his trucks on the floor in front of us. My husband was still at work and we were enjoying a quiet afternoon. I was starting to think about dinner, trying to remember what we had in the freezer upstairs when Laura shrieked.

I looked up in time to see the back door in the basement fly open. At the same time, a dark figure darted past the window outside.

I stood up, uncertainty freezing me in my steps.

What if it was an intruder?

"Shut the door!" Laura screamed, causing me to lunge forward. I ran across the room and pushed the door closed, sliding the deadlock bolt in place for extra measure.

I stared out into the yard, not knowing what to do. From where I stood, I could see the entire back yard. If someone ran past, he would have to cross fifty yards of open space to reach the nearest hiding place.

I herded the children upstairs on the pretense of starting dinner, but inside I was still quaking. How could I pass that off as anything but paranormal? Laura saw it for herself.

I pulled a package of chicken nuggets from the freezer, no longer having the energy to prepare a detailed meal. As I filled a pot with water for the macaroni and cheese we'd have with the nuggets, Laura asked the question I'd been dreading.

"Mom, do we have a ghost in our house?" she asked.

I turned the water off and sat the pot down in the sink. There were some things I could shield her from, but this was no longer an option.

"I'm not sure what it is," I told her truthfully. Her father and I had extensive conversations about not telling her about Gus until we were safely away from the house, but now the cat was out of the bag.

"I've seen things in my room at night," she told me.

My blood ran cold. I had no idea that Gus was affecting her. I thought he was only out for me.

Years later, Trevor would tell me about a time he tried to reach something on the upper shelf of the refrigerator. Since he was too short, he couldn't reach it, so he decided to climb the shelves. As he stepped up, he felt an invisible hand lift him up, allowing him to grab onto the item before it gently put him back down.

Apparently, Gus had softened because of the children.
Now, he wasn't planning on letting us go.

Things would only get worse from there.

(Above) Laura, Joni, Trevor, and Joni's father, Harold

26

As soon as we listed the house with a real estate agency, I drove to Oakham and enrolled the kids in their new schools.

I loved the town and the quiet country feeling it had. Even though we would have to drive ten miles to the nearest grocery store, it still felt like home. I imagined us building our dream house and living there happily ever after. Gus had other ideas.

People began coming to view the house. All the work we did made the house a showplace. Gone was the feeling of neglect, with the worn down appliances and dirty walls. In its place was a beautiful Georgian Colonial with gleaming hardwood floors and bright spaces.

I thought that we would sell it immediately, but no offers came in.

"People are worried about the unfinished bathrooms on the second floor," the realtor told us.

I was fairly certain that wasn't all they were worried about.

I could feel Gus lingering at the corners of the room when people came to look at the house. If he made his presence known to me, he must have also reached out to them as well. Potential buyers would stare across the room, crinkling their noses as though they smelled something foul.

The house was as perfect as I could make it with two children and a dog. Buddy and Sheba both died the previous year, but we only went several months before my husband came home from work with a beautiful German Shepard puppy.

Shelby was well behaved from the beginning. It took very little training to teach her the rules of the house.

When people came to view the house, we put her in the backyard, away from the commotion. What they were sensing was beyond their five senses.

I began having nightmares again.

In them, the man who chased me often caught me, telling me he would never allow me to leave. We were his and he was never letting us go. I woke with a scream on my lips, echoed by the sound of my daughter's screams down the hallway as she was caught in her own nightmare.

"You have to let us leave," I begged him. "New people will move in. Maybe you'll like them," I said.

I could feel his anger swirl through the room.

It made me fearful of what he might do in retaliation.

It started with the dog.

Shelby was an agreeable dog, preferring to spend her time with the kids, playing, or chewing on a bone. She was content with her new home until the moment we put the house up for sale. Then she started running away.

I watched her in the backyard, going from board to board on the picket fence until she found one she could pry loose. She darted through the gap and was gone in a heartbeat.

Tracking her down became a daily chore. For reasons unknown to me, I always found her in the subdivision across the woods from our house, sitting on the porch of a million-dollar home.

"She must be trying to upgrade," my husband said jokingly. The truth was a bit harder to handle. I think Gus was getting to her, as well.

She began getting explosive diarrhea the minute prospective buyers showed up at the door. Once, she soiled the basement stairs from top to bottom, filling the house with a noxious stench.

148

I took her to the vet, but nothing was wrong with her. We changed her to a bland diet, but her stomach still became upset when people came to view the house.

"Maybe, it just upsets her," someone suggested, but I wasn't convinced. I thought there was more to it.

I wouldn't see the full extent to Gus's wrath until we finally got an offer on the house. A family from India was interested in buying it and sealed the deal with a small deposit.

I was overjoyed and began packing. Over the course of the next three months, we nearly had the entire house boxed up. The children were looking forward to starting school in their new town and friends were planning a party in our honor.

As I wrapped glassware with newspaper and placed it in a box, the phone rang. It was our realtor

The new owners withdrew their offer.

We were back to square one.

(Above) Shelby the German Shepard

27

The house became dark again. Gone was the light of the past few years and the happiness that accompanied it. The children began bickering incessantly and my husband often came home in a foul mood. I found myself sinking into a pit of depression. Everything we worked for was falling apart. We would be stuck in this house forever.

I began to hate the house and everything it represented. It held us back from moving forward with our lives as it caused me to plunge into the darkest, deepest hole I've ever been in.

"I hate you!" I screamed at the walls, listening to the sounds of the house surrounding me.

I knew every noise by heart. The click of the heater as it purred to life, the drip of the tub faucet if it was wasn't turned off tightly, and the creak of the wind as it pushed against the siding.

I knew how to latch the screen door so it wouldn't fly open with the first gust of wind. I knew the colors of the paint, the dimensions of the windows and the number of treads on the solid oak staircase. I could walk down to the basement and show you where the writing on the wall appeared and where the old workbench once stood, but I couldn't tell you why the ghost was keeping us here.

He hated us in the beginning and made our lives hell, but then he reconsidered and decided not to let us leave.

I sent the kids to a neighbor's house for the afternoon as I took the long drive to Oakham to unenroll the kids from their new school. As I passed under the canopy of bright green leaves, I felt the loss like a bruise on my soul.

I cried all the way back to my hell house. My eyes were swollen and red as I pushed the key in the door and walked through the front door.

"You won, you bastard," I whispered to the air itself, knowing that Gus was around. He was always around.

That's what he did best.

(Above) The house while it was up for sale

28

We pulled the house off the real estate market at the end of the summer. Even if we had an offer, we didn't have time to find a place to live in Oakham.

My husband made the call to the developer, who gave us our deposit back on the plot of land that was a perfect fit for us, while I enrolled the kids back into the school system I had hoped to leave behind.

"We'll finish the bathrooms over the winter. Maybe then it will sell," he said.

I nodded, not having the energy to follow through with a response. We were barely making enough money to live on. Putting more money into the house seemed like a massive undertaking. I couldn't imagine getting excited about it.

As the holidays closed in on us, we hunkered down and made the best of it. On the weekends, we worked on the bathrooms, spending as little as possible to finish them. By the time the new millennium rolled out, we were beyond tired.

I spent my weekends and evenings working at a local steakhouse, putting in agonizingly long hours running food to tables and smiling when I felt like crying instead. As the clock ticked towards midnight on New Year's Eve, my boss at the steakhouse let me leave for the night, giving me precisely ten full minutes to make my way home.

I didn't end up making it, which was just as well. I watched the clock on my car dashboard click over to midnight as I sat at a stoplight in the middle of Westborough. I arrived home to find my husband waiting. While he felt bad for me, having to work on the biggest New Year's Eve of our lives, there really wasn't much to celebrate.

We thought we would have spent it in our new house in Oakham, toasting each other for surviving the past ten years and for escaping. Instead, we were here.

By the time February rolled around, the bathrooms were finished and we put the house back on the real estate market.

I thought about what Bree's boyfriend told me about claiming my space. Didn't I have the same rights with my life?

I waited until Laura was at school and Trevor was at preschool before I walked back into the house alone.

I paced up and down the long hallway, the same place I once logged several hundred footsteps with my colicky babies. When I stopped in the dining room, where the linoleum was once cracked and peeling, I stood and waited for him to find me.

"We gave you ten years," I told him, listening until I finally heard the ringing sound grow closer. "But that doesn't mean you can force us to stay. I don't want to live here any longer. I want to move. You must release us," I told him.

In the silence, I heard nothing more than the continued ringing of my ears.

He heard me, but that didn't mean anything.

The choice was still his to make.

Either he released us or he didn't.

One thing was for certain. He might be a thief of my happiness, but he could never have my soul. That was the one thing I refused to give him.

We sold the house a week later.

29

We moved to Oakham that summer and lived in our camper in a nearby campground while our house was being built. It was one of the greatest summers of my life.

The kids played with the other children at the campground, making friends they kept through adulthood. I walked the two mile distance to the new house every day, checking on the progress and marveling at the beauty of the woods surrounding our dream home.

We moved in at the end of October, as the first snowstorm of the season blew in from the west. Snow fell in buckets as we celebrated with pizza and movies in our new living room, while our camper sat empty in the yard.

My nightmares and sleepwalking stopped altogether, as did my daughters.

I'd like to say we lived happily ever after, but such things seldom exist. The damage our marriage suffered at the Westborough house was long lasting and sustaining. We only endured for another five years before it all ended.

I packed my things once more and set out for an unknown that was still unwritten. My family was shattered into pieces, and we were scattered to the wind, but we survived.

My daughter remained with her father, while my son split his time between the two houses, and now lives with me full time while he goes to college. My daughter put herself through college to become a nuclear engineer. She now works at a naval shipyard, proving to me that I was right all along. She could take care of herself with no problem.

My ex-husband married within a few years to his high school sweetheart, living across town from our old house in Oakham.

I'm still alone ten years later, but I'm not unhappy. I have my son, my pets, my writing, and most of all my soul.

Everything happens for a reason.
I still believe that.
I always will.

(Above) the dream house in Oakham

30

Nearly ten years to the day that we moved out, I took a drive down the familiar streets of Westborough. So much had changed in the years since we left, but so much was the same, as well.

I saw the duplex at the end of the street where my friend Debbie once lived with her family. Different children played in the yard, which gave me a touch of melancholy.

Debbie and her three children used to come to my house frequently when Trevor was small. I remembered the children playing in the sandbox in the back yard while Debbie and I chatted. She was the first real friend I'd had in years.

The street was still narrow and bumpy and the traffic continued to drive too fast. It made me remember standing at the edge of my lawn, watching over my children as I encouraged the cars to slow down. I paused as I passed the corner where the school bus always stopped to pick up my daughter.

Images played through my head of her swirling in the princess dress she insisted upon wearing to school one day and of the bright smile that played across her face.

I rolled to a stop when I saw the house.

Not much had changed about it. It was still a grey two-story Georgian Colonial with a picket fence surrounding the side yard. The bushes were overgrown, but they were the same bushes from before. Even the tree we planted when Laura was born was alive. Instead of the sapling I remembered, it now towered high into the sky, providing shade for the side yard.

I didn't linger long enough for Gus to find me at the curb. The last thing I wanted was for him to follow me home to my new place. I had enough of living in the devil's toy box. I put my car back into drive and continued down the narrow residential area.

In the end, I stopped seeing Gus as a negative entity and started seeing him as a person.

His name was probably Bob. He was a hard-working man with a life he despised. He spent most of his time down in the basement, working on projects and putting a well-needed distance between him and his wife.

He died of a heart attack in the room we used as a bedroom for many years. He must have stuck around to watch over his wife and his house. When his wife moved to a nursing home and eventually died herself, all he had left was his house.

After we left, it apparently took him a while to find a family he liked. I heard from neighbors that the house sold five times in five years.

I felt horrible for the legacy we left behind, but it was all we could do at the time. Saving ourselves was our top priority.

Maybe one day, I'll return to set him free.

Then, we'll all have the peace we deserve.

The End

Please continue reading for a preview of Joni's next paranormal experience, The Soul Collector.

The Soul Collector

Joni Mayhan

The true story of one paranormal investigator's worst nightmare.

The Soul Collector

By

Joni Mayhan

Chapter 1

I was warned to never talk about him.

I was supposed to just walk away and forget the entire experience, totally erasing him from my memory. If I didn't, there was a very good chance he could come back to find me again. I held onto this story for several years, trying to follow their advice, but I just couldn't.

I needed to tell my story.

I wasn't in a very good place when he found me. I was at the end of a two-year relationship with someone I thought I would spend the rest of my life with, growing old together. When he walked away so suddenly, it left my whole life in shambles.

With my entire family living a thousand miles away, I didn't have anyone to turn to. I'm not the kind of person who cries to other people about her problems. I swallowed the pain whole, and then allowed it to consume me. It burrowed and spread, reaching into every cell of my being, leaving me nothing more than a shell.

I was forty-seven years old, living in a small house in the rural town of Barre, Massachusetts. I purchased the nine-hundred square foot ranch house after my divorce in 2005, hoping to find a place to rest before moving onto my happily-ever-after. Six years later, I was in the same place with no hope in sight.

After spending weeks locked inside my house with the curtains drawn, I finally decided to get out and do something. People told me that staying busy was the best cure for a broken heart, so I tried.

A friend invited me to go ghost hunting. As it turns out, it was the worst thing I could have done. It brought me to the Soul Collector.

(Below: Joni investigating in the basement of one of her favorite haunted locations.

Chapter 2

I got into ghost hunting quite by accident.

I spent a solid three years after my divorce hiding out in my house. I didn't have any friends to speak of and had nowhere to go. Besides, people were hurtful and scary. I preferred spending the time with my pets or by myself, writing, reading, and watching movies.

Sometimes I feel like a hopeless cause. I've never been socially adept. Since grade school, I've had a difficult time interacting with my peers. Being small as a child, I was often picked on by schoolyard bullies. I didn't fare much better in high school. It seemed like every time I allowed myself to get close to someone, I ended up getting hurt. In the end, I decided it was better to just be alone and save myself the pain. It turned out to be a lonely decision that I would soon reconsider.

The one friend I retained into adulthood was actually an old high-school boyfriend who still lived in Indiana. Finding ourselves both single after years of marriage, we forged a long-distance friendship. John was the one who got me to come out of my shell. First, he talked me into setting up an online dating profile.

Initially, I was almost giddy with all the attention I was suddenly getting. After going for days without seeing another soul, I was being invited out onto dates with eligible men. John was doing the same thing back in Indiana and we started using one another as sounding boards.

"I need a woman's point of view," he'd say, then ask me a question. I'd offer my best advice, eventually helping him connect with his soon-to-be wife Melinda. I'd run situations and concerns past him for a man's point of view.

We spent many long nights on the phone just chatting and helping each other through the hard times. "You need to get out of your house," he told me one day. "Why don't you look into Meetup.com? Find something you like on there." He'd found a kayaking group there and enjoyed the occasional weekend outing with a group of people who shared his love of the water. He suggested I look into it to see if I could find a ghost hunting group, knowing how much I was into the paranormal.

While I had never investigated before, I was well versed on the subject. I'd spent the past few years amassing quite a collection of books on the paranormal. I read them from cover to cover, over and over again. I understood the difference between a residual haunting and an intelligent spirit. I was intrigued by the concept of EVPs, and even had my own digital recorder to record spirit voices. It was time to put my knowledge to work.

I took John's advice and quickly found a paranormal meet-up group. I signed up for their next event and waited eagerly for the day to arrive.

The first event was a wash out. The people who ran the event were a flaky bunch. They set up a meet-up at the Hoosic Tunnel in North Adams, Massachusetts.

Spanning over five miles, the tunnel snakes through the base of the Berkshire Mountains, cutting a path that was paved by bloodshed and death. People who dared enter it sometimes found themselves in the company of ghosts. Other people were smart enough not to walk several miles into a tunnel where an active train tunnel runs.

I had no doubt that the tunnel contained residual energy. The ground and stone have a tendency to absorb the vibrations from traumatic events in the past, replaying them like a movie, over and over again. A good example of this is Gettysburg. You can't walk out onto a battlefield without feeling the hair on the back of your neck prickle. It's as though Mother Earth is telling you, "Something happened here." People often see soldiers, or hear cannon fire, as history replays itself, but they seldom make contact with the apparitions.

While residual hauntings were interesting, making contact with an intelligent spirit was my overall goal. I had high hopes for the Hoosic Tunnel.

I brought my twenty-year-old daughter, Laura, with me to the event. We were both appropriately nervous about venturing inside. As we walked down the tracks leading to the tunnel, I could feel the anticipation rapidly turn to anxiety.

"What if a train comes?" I asked my daughter, eyeing the narrow space between the tracks and the stone walls. We might be able to press ourselves against the sides and hope for the best, but it sounded horrifically dangerous.

Laura shrugged. Suddenly, it didn't seem like such a great idea.

Several members of the meet-up group were gathered near the tunnel entrance. As we approached them, we could feel the air grow colder by several degrees.

"I'm glad to see you brought jackets," an older woman said to us. "It's quite a bit colder inside the tunnel," she said.

After quick introductions, we learned that she was the meet-up leader.

Something about her truly gave me the creeps. I wasn't sure if it was the way she looked, with her mop of unbrushed hair, or the way she was dressed in layers of skirts and shawls, accessorized by thick sandals with socks. It may have just been the wild look in her eyes that made me think of an escaped mental patient. Either way, she made me uncomfortable.

She had two other investigators with her. One was a younger woman who was the equipment expert. She walked around with an EMF meter in her hand. The other was a tall, thin man, who just stood back and watched.

"Are you getting anything?" I asked the younger woman.

"No. Nothing so far," she told me, showing me her EMF meter.

My daughter gave me a curious look, so I explained what an EMF meter does.

"It measures changes in the electro-magnetic field in an area. If a ghost comes close to us, we might see a spike in the reading," I told her. While I was anxious to have a paranormal experience, I hoped it would be a little more substantial than a blip on someone's meter.

I took my digital recorder out of my pocket and started recording, hoping for an EVP. I showed it to my daughter.

"When a ghost speaks to us, we usually can't hear them. But, if you are recording it with a digital recorder, you might record their response. It's called an EVP: electronic voice phenomena."

I asked a few questions, and then listened to the audio, hearing nothing but silence. I was disappointed, but was still hopeful. If we tried it again inside the tunnel, we might have better results.

We lingered near the entrance for several minutes. The others were milling around, talking. I was ready to go inside and get started. "Are we going in?" I finally asked.

The leader turned to look at me, her face frozen with fright. "No. I can't go in there. This place is sheer evil," she said, hopefully not noticing when I rolled my eyes.

"So, what are we going to do?" I asked, growing appropriately agitated. We paid ten dollars apiece for the experience, but we weren't going in?

"You can go in, if you want to," the leader said. "But, I'm staying right here." Her team members stuck to her side, refusing to budge as well.

I sighed and looked around, wondering what to do. It was a beautiful blue-sky day in early May. The leaves were just popping out on the trees, and the air was filled with the sweet scent of spring. We'd driven nearly two hours to be there. It seemed a shame to waste the trip only to just turn around and leave.

I turned to my daughter. "Wanna go in a little ways?" I asked.

"Might as well," she said, without much enthusiasm.

We'd spent eleven years living in a haunted house. While we were both curious about the paranormal, we were both a little apprehensive. Sometimes opening a door to something brings you closer than you anticipated.

I'd read that ghosts often drained the batteries on your equipment, so I was well prepared for the walk. I'd put fresh batteries into four flashlights. I gave two to my daughter and kept the other two for myself. There was no way I was going to be submerged in the darkness with no light. It just wasn't going to happen.

As we were getting ready to walk in, three men joined us at the mouth of the tunnel. The oldest man was obviously the father of one of the younger men. They wanted to check out the tunnel but didn't have a flashlight. Not really thinking, I offered to let them follow us.

I should preface this with the fact that I am a little too trusting of others, at least at first. Sometimes my common sense takes a backseat to my willingness to please. It's a fault I will find myself making over and over in my life.

I walked in first, with my daughter behind me, and the three men trailing along behind us.

The tunnel was eerie. The minute we walked inside, the darkness quickly enveloped us with cold, damp fingers. I shined my light around, trying to get a feel for the place.

The tall, curved ceilings were lined with bricks. Many of the bricks had fallen, which was evident from the broken shards at our feet. Graffiti graced nearly every wall like strange artwork.

The tracks were difficult to walk on and water dripped from the ceilings, creating echoes through the tunnel. After walking for ten minutes, we were deep in the heart of the mountain. I turned around, surprised to find the tunnel opening no more than a tiny circle, floating in the darkness behind us.

It suddenly occurred to me what I was doing. I willingly led my beautiful daughter into a dark tunnel with three men I didn't know. While they seemed normal, I had no idea of their intent. My active imagination went into overdrive. What if they were bad men? I didn't think that serial killers usually hunted in packs, but who really knew?

"Ummm....you guys aren't serial killers," I said, trying to make it sound like a joke.

There was a long silence before one of the men finally spoke.

"I guess it's a little late to be asking that question, isn't it?" one of them said. He had a smile in his voice when he said it, but my discomfort level was already rising into the red zone.

"Let's turn around," I suggested, praying they wouldn't take that moment to reveal some evil personalities.

Forgetting all about my desire to do another EVP session, we turned around and made our way out of the tunnel in record time. Thankfully, the men were nothing more than true gentlemen and we parted ways at the mouth of the tunnel. I just stood there as they walked back towards the parking lot, feeling very foolish.

"What a stupid thing to do," I whispered to my daughter. I was so angry with myself for putting her in possible danger. If a train didn't run us over, the strangers could have turned out to be something other than just nice, ordinary men. What kind of mother was I?

I didn't have long to berate myself, because the meet-up leader was quickly approaching.

"Did you feel anything?" she asked, wide-eyed.

I was embarrassed she was even asking me. Admitting that I *did* or *didn't* feel something felt like social suicide. What if someone heard us? They'd think I was just as crazy as she was.

Honestly, the only thing I felt was the sense of intrigue followed by the rush of overwhelming fear. I wasn't afraid of ghosts. I was afraid of the men walking behind us and the situation I'd put us in. We nearly ran back to the car.

It would be several years later before I'd try it again.

The Soul Collector can be found at Amazon.com and at BarnesandNoble.com in eBook format or paperback.

http://www.amazon.com/Soul-Collector-Joni-Mayhan-ebook/dp/B00EIHG90Q/ref=sr_1_1?ie=UTF8&qid=1424556650&sr=8-1&keywords=joni+mayhan

(Below) Joni's daughter Laura, at the Hoosic Tunnel

Devil's Toy Box

About the author

Joni Mayhan grew up in southern Indiana on forty acres of lush farmland. Many of her stories borrow from the landscape of her youth, a place where her imagination grew wings. Joni now lives in western Massachusetts with her son Trevor and a houseful of spoiled pets. She also has a daughter named Laura who lives in Maine and works as a nuclear engineer. Joni is a seasoned paranormal investigator who spends her spare time in dark abandoned places talking to the dead.

For more information about Joni, please visit her website: jonimayhan.com

CPSIA information can be obtained at www.ICGtesting.com
Printed in the USA
BVOW08s1145200415

396888BV00003B/7/P

9 781508 448976